W9-ACJ-003

Gramley Library
Salem Academy and College
Winston-Salem, N.C. 27108

HWARCHIN

Farlanburg Stories

91-249

PS
3561
.O354
F37
1990

Farlanburg Stories

Lisa Koger

W·W· Norton & Company

New York · London

Gramley Library
Salem Academy and College
Winston-Salem, N.C. 27108

Grateful acknowledgment is made to the publications in which some of these stories previously appeared: "The June Woman" in *Seventeen*, June 1985; "Bypass" in *Kennesaw Review*, Fall 1987 and in *American Voice*, Winter 1987; "Baby Luv" in *Kennesaw Review*, Fall 1987; and "The Retirement Party" in *Ploughshares* 16, no. 1.

Copyright © 1990 by Lisa Koger
All rights reserved.
Printed in the United States of America.

The text of this book is composed in Century Old Style, with display type set in Century Nova. Composition and manufacturing by Haddon Craftsmen Inc.
Book design by Charlotte Staub.

First Edition

Library of Congress Cataloging-in-Publication Data

Koger, Lisa.
  Farlanburg stories/Lisa Koger.
    p. cm.
  ISBN 0-393-02856-9
  I. Title.
  PS3561.0354F37 1990
  813'.54—dc20   89–25501

ISBN 0-393-02856-9

W.W. Norton & Company, Inc.
500 Fifth Avenue, New York, N.Y. 10110
W.W. Norton & Company, Ltd.
37 Great Russell Street, London WC1B3NU

1 2 3 4 5 6 7 8 9 0

For Muzz and Koger

Contents

Acknowledgments

I would like to thank Sallie Bingham and the Kentucky Foundation for Women and James Michener and the Copernicus Society of America for support during the writing of this book. I would also like to thank Jane Gelfman, Gerry Howard, Madison Bell, and Allan Gurganus for encouragement and good advice, and Jane Hill, Diane Neill, Robin Finesmith, and Brian Kologe for their time and careful reading.

Farlanburg Stories

Gramley Library
Salem Academy and College
Winston-Salem, N.C. 27108

Bypass

Friday night and Earl has a taste for chicken. The craving slipped up on him, fox-like, sometime late in the afternoon. Tonight, he doesn't want Ruth's Crispy or Wanda's Golden Fried or chicken from any of the other joints in town. He doesn't want chain-food chicken from one of those bright new places on the bypass, either. It scares him to eat at places where there are signs that tell him billions have eaten the same thing. There's more than safety in numbers, he knows.

What he really has a taste for is home-fried chicken. The kind his mother made. Earl's mother has been dead almost twenty years. She wasn't an outstanding cook or an especially clean one. She dripped sweat on the plates and scratched her legs with her butcher knives. But she knew the importance of feeding a man.

"You're a helluva good woman," Earl wishes he'd said to her just once, but he didn't. Appreciation is a bonus given to the dead. Now that Earl's approaching middle age himself, he'd settle for half what's coming to him if he could only have it early.

At the stoplight on Main Street in downtown Farlanburg, he signals left and heads north on Route 19 out of town. School's just let out, and the streets are filled with yellow buses beginning their routes. Earl recognizes most of the faces behind the bus windows because he teaches those faces for a living. In Farlanburg, a man can farm if he has one, teach if he doesn't, or drive a truck for Hallawell Chemical Company and get cancer by the time he's fifty. All three jobs will kill him. It's a matter of how long he wants to linger.

He stops at the Bi-Lo and gets some chicken—a family pack, bulging with breasts, legs, and thighs. He plans to drop by the ceramic shop where his wife, Brenda, works and see if he can talk her into coming home and frying it up for him. Chicken is not the only thing he'd like to talk her into, but given the state of things between them, he figures chicken is as good a place as any to start.

Something is wrong with Earl's marriage but not with Brenda's. When he tries to talk to her about it, she looks at him as if he's just told her his athlete's foot has come back. This is a personal problem, her look says. Why are you discussing this with me?

Brenda doesn't discuss personal problems. She prefers to keep busy instead. During the past three years, she and Earl have enclosed the carport, knocked out a side wall to enlarge the living room, replaced the kitchen cabinets, and built a deck that wraps around three sides of their three-bedroom house. They did most of the work themselves, and it looks it. On weekends, when Earl runs down to the hardware store for more paneling or nails, Lonnie, who works in home repairs, slaps him on the back and tells him he's the busiest man he knows. Earl agrees, but he doesn't know *why* he's so busy. He saw nothing wrong with the house in the first place.

"Maybe not," says Brenda, "but it doesn't pay to have too much time to sit around and think."

Earl will be forty come September, and he *wants* to think. He knows he's not the man he was at eighteen, but there's nothing wrong with his ears. He hears something eating away at his happiness just as surely as he hears mice gnawing inside Brenda's kitchen cabinets at night.

Mice aren't the only things gnawing away at Earl's house. There are Kivetts. The Kivetts are Brenda's people. Strange rangers, the Kivetts. They come to Earl's house, eat his steak, and treat him like he's not at home.

"They're just quiet," Brenda says. "You tell me what you want them to say, and I'll make sure they do."

Earl isn't sure what he wants from the Kivetts, including Brenda. Whatever he wants, it seems to be too much.

Tonight is steak and Kivett night at Earl's house. Every Friday night is steak and Kivett night at Earl's house. It's been that way for most of the last fifteen years. Earl can afford steak if he's careful, but it's still a luxury to him. He hates putting something as special as steak into the mouths of people as unspecial as the Kivetts.

Usually, it's the mister and missus. Sometimes Brenda's sister, Mary, comes, too. Mary is forty-one and has been brain-damaged since birth. She wears pigtails, has blue eyes, and lets her mama dress her in a different shade of anklets every day of the week. The real giveaway is Mary's disposition. She's *so* happy. More so, Earl thinks, than any normal adult could possibly be.

Earl is jealous of Mary's happiness, but he likes her. Some-

times he thinks there's nothing really wrong with her at all—
that she's playing some sly, accommodating sort of game.
Other times, he's sure she's a prophet with a message she's
waiting to deliver.

At any rate, Mary fills Earl with hope. He never knows
when she's going to do something that will help him remember how to laugh or say something that says more than she
means. He long ago gave up expecting such things from
Brenda or the mister and missus.

"I don't know what you want from me," Brenda says whenever Earl complains. She looks at him and blinks. Her face is a
closed door. "Do Not Disturb," the sign says.

Earl has learned to keep quiet, but inside his head, a steady
drip tells him life is not supposed to be like this.

Earl stops at the shop to see if Brenda will
knock off early and come home with him. The place is hot and
packed. Women are jammed shoulder to shoulder around the
tables, smoking, scraping and sanding frogs and miniature
Christmas trees. It's eight months until Christmas.

Brenda is timing a load of ginger jars in her "oven" and
painting eyes on a unicorn for a friend. She works with the
intensity of a woman who's just discovered what she does
best. "Don't forget to glaze the bottom of your salt and pep-
per shakers, Kimberly Jean," she says to a woman across the
table. "Loved that decal you used on your chamber pot."

Brenda's been in the ceramics business almost three years.
At first, she got ticked off when Earl called her kiln an oven.
"It's a kiln, Earl honey," she said. "How do you expect people
to take me serious if you go around calling my kiln an oven?"
She doesn't get ticked off anymore. She doesn't call Earl
"honey," either. To get ticked off at someone or call him
"honey," you have to have feelings for him, and Brenda

seems to have lost all hers for Earl. Her mouth hasn't said the words. Her body does the talking. "You leave me cold as a snake," it says. Earl isn't sure what he's done wrong, but judging by the way Mrs. Kivett treats the mister, he must've done the same thing.

"What're you doing here?" Brenda says when Earl walks in. "I thought you were gonna get the steaks and come pick me up at five." She glances at her watch. "It ain't anywheres near five." Brenda wears her blonde hair short and curly like a poodle's. She's still a good-looking woman, but at thirty-eight, she's beginning to get that look that says, "I bite."

Earl looks at his watch like the time is news to him.

"What you got in that sack, Earl?" Melanie Woodford asks. "He's so sweet," she says to the others. "He's brought her something."

"What you got, Earl?" a couple of women chime in.

Earl drifts toward Brenda's table. "Nothing. Just a chicken." He shrugs and lays it on a window sill.

"He's brought her a chicken." Someone laughs.

"I told you it was nothing," Earl says to Brenda, who is not laughing.

The women return to their scraping, and Earl pulls up a chair behind Brenda. "How much longer do you think you'll be here?" he whispers.

"Hard to tell," she replies in a voice that, to Earl, is unnecessarily loud.

He scoots his chair closer, crowding against some greenware shelves. "How about quitting early this evening and coming home with me? We'll fry chicken together and talk. Just look at this," he says, reaching for the sack. He pulls the chicken out and whistles with approval. "What a bird! We'll have fun. Just the two of us. We'll fix a nice supper and have it ready by the time the girls get home."

Brenda touches up one eye of her unicorn. "Mama and Daddy are coming by at six for steaks. You know that."

"Call 'em. Tell 'em we can't do it this evening," Earl says quietly. We'll fix this chicken. Just you and me. Like it used to be."

Brenda looks up. "Don't lean against those shelves thataway, Earl. You bust up any of my greenware, and the girls'll ride you outa here on a rail. Ain't that right, Edna?" she says to the woman on her left. Edna is a big woman with red knuckles and little eyes. She looks like she does ceramics only when she can't find a fight.

Earl nods. He puts the chicken in the sack, then scoots his chair away from the shelves. He clasps and unclasps his hands and looks at the floor like a benched player watching his team lose the game. "Tell you what," he finally says, resting his elbows on his knees. He's aware that every ear in the room is listening. "I'll go in there to the phone right now and call 'em. OK? What good's a phone if you can't use it at a time like this." He looks at the women and laughs, but it sounds like a bark. "I'm gonna go in there, ring 'em up, and say, real nice, that it's nothing against 'em, but that my wife and I want to be alone and fix chicken by ourselves tonight. They'll understand. Most people would understand that. What do you say?"

Brenda tilts her head to the side as though she is considering the matter. "Edna honey," she finally says. "Your soup bowl has seams up the sides that are gonna need sanding. Hand me a piece of that green scour pad, why don't you, and I'll show you how to rub it down real good."

The speed limit on the bypass is fifty-five. Earl's doing forty. He could do twice that and get away with it because the Farlanburg police don't come out here.

People in Farlanburg didn't want the bypass, but you couldn't go so far as to say they were against it. Those who had something to sell were the exceptions. They were afraid the bypass would hurt their business. They were right. Hardest hit were the Tumblin girls in tight polyester pants who did business from the rock wall at the north end of town. They counted on the caravans of trucks that passed through.

Others, who sold something more legitimate, have spent too much on advertising to postpone the inevitable. Their gaudy signs have sprung up overnight. "Sleep cheap! Kids eat free! Mom too!"

Earl didn't want the bypass, and he has nothing to sell. He's suspicious of people who spend millions of dollars to take him around something when he can see more by passing through.

He grew up in this section of the county in a white frame house that isn't white anymore. It's bright yellow and, thanks to the bypass, sits about three hundred feet from where it used to. Earl's sister still lives there. This evening, he feels the need to drive out to see her. He's not going to see her as much as he is to see himself, he knows, the way he used to be. He wants to sit in the paneled living room, sip a Coke, and look at pictures of himself when he was young and sure that the best was still ahead.

He remembers when there was nothing out here but fields, farmhouses, and a barn every now and then. He used to cut through those fields on rainy Sunday afternoons just to lie in the hayloft of the barn with "See Rock City" painted on its side. "See Rock Cit-y, See Rock Cit-y," the rain said as the drops hit the roof, ran down the tin, and dug holes in the manure below. He would lie in the hay, eat ham and mustard sandwiches, and plan his life the way he wanted it to be: college (out of state, of course), a stint in the army where he'd prove himself in Ranger school or in the Special Forces. He'd sign on as a mercenary after that. Spend a couple of years in the jungles of some foreign country. Then back to the U.S. of A. and someplace like Houston or San Francisco, a good job, good wife, and a couple of kids.

When he was sixteen, he and a friend, Bucky Eads, pooled their money and bought a car. A '61 Dodge with no muffler and rusted tailfins. They drove to Chattanooga one weekend to see Rock City.

"Somebody lied. It wasn't half what it's cracked up to be," Earl kept saying as they drove home that night, headlights flashing across his face.

"Doesn't matter," Bucky said.

But to Earl it did. He wouldn't be sixteen forever, he told himself. He'd have a job. Money to travel. He'd see places that'd make Rock City look sick.

He stayed in town to go to college. Figured he'd save money by going to Farlanburg State. He planned to clear out the day after graduation.

During his junior year, he started dating Brenda. He'd known her since high school when she was Wayne Sayer's girl and so good-looking she wouldn't give him the time of day. By this time, she was Wayne Sayer's ex with two kids to raise, and she was willing to give Earl anything he wanted. She gave it so willingly and so well that Earl forgot his plans. He graduated, married Brenda, and decided that the rest could wait.

Kim and Kerry, Brenda's girls, are seventeen and eighteen. They have red hair like their daddy, linebacker faces, and give no indication they'll ever leave home. They giggle and poke each other whenever Earl is in the same room. He has never been a religious man, but he's a grateful one. He gives thanks every night that those girls have never asked to call him "Daddy."

So Earl is back at Farlanburg High with the feeling he never really left. He teaches history and American government to kids who don't want to know about either. They want to smoke behind the lunchroom, jump up and down at pep rallies, and rub against each other in front of the lockers. Some days, Earl is tempted to tell them things he didn't learn in college. He'd start by saying he's older than he ever planned to be.

Home has never felt the same to Earl since the house was moved. Without concrete walks or flowers around the porch, it looks like it just fell out of the sky and landed in the field one night.

Earl's sister, Trudy, drives the bookmobile for the library, and she doesn't have time for flowers like her mother used to. She doesn't understand the need for them, either. "Imagine getting all worked up over a marigold!" she often says, wrinkling her nose and curling her upper lip like a horse.

Trudy has never been married, but she'd like to be. Part of the reason she hasn't is that she'd *very much* like to be. When she was in high school, she was president of the Future Homemakers of America, and she and her girlfriends used to spend Saturday afternoons looking at engagement rings in Hurt's Jewelry store window. They had visions of tree-lined streets, Hotpoint stoves, and everlasting marital bliss.

Most of Trudy's friends got married. On the rare occasions when she sees them in town on Saturday mornings, they dash from their cars to the grocery store, then to Murphy's to pick up something for their kids. They remind her of locust shells, she once told Earl—brittle, empty versions of the people they used to be. Sometimes, she thinks they avoid her because she isn't married. Other times, she could swear they are signaling to her to stay away, trying to warn her about something with their weary, sunken eyes.

Earl parks his car in the yard, which is nothing more than a small square of orchard grass that Trudy's been mowing. He picks up the chicken. It's bled through the sack and onto the seat. He stares at the spot, rubs it, then gets out.

Birds swoop from the roof to the power line as he walks toward the porch. Peepers sing from the ditch behind the house. Earl knocks loudly, waits, then knocks again. "Anybody home?" he yells, opening the door and stepping inside. The house is quiet. He puts the chicken in the kitchen sink.

"Trudy?" He hears a stirring in one of the back rooms as though something has just come to life, then the ssstt, ssstt, ssstt, ssstt of slippers on the hallway linoleum.

"Earl?"

"It's me."

Trudy pokes her head through the curtains at the entrance to the hallway and looks suspiciously around the room.

"I'm alone. Brenda had to work late," Earl says.

"Law, that woman of yours goes after it, don't she?" Trudy steps from behind the curtains. "It's just as well this evening. I don't want anybody seeing me looking like this." Her hands move self-consciously over her stomach and thighs. "I'm bloated. Must have been something I ate."

"Maybe you're pregnant."

Trudy snorts and waves her hand, but she continues to watch Earl's face to see if he's going to laugh at the idea. She has put on a lot of weight since high school and might easily be mistaken for a woman in her second trimester. Her bobbed hair sticks up in the back, and a pillow or cover has left a red tatoo on the side of her face. She has the dream-swollen look of a woman who sleeps too much.

"I woke you up," Earl says.

"No, you didn't. I was just resting my eyes."

Despite the fact that it's mid-April and warm enough for wasps and bees, Trudy's gas heater is going full blast. Parched plants sit on a table near the window, their yellow, leafless stems skewed toward the light. The world outside looks fuzzy and unfocused because the plastic on the windows hasn't been taken down.

Trudy scoots a footstool toward the heater and motions Earl to the couch. She rubs her forehead, then fiddles with her hair. "I don't know what's got into me," she says. "I come home from work, and I'm so tired. Today I was just gonna rest my feet and legs for a spell, and the next thing I know, I look up, and it's two hours later, and I hear someone banging around the house. I have to slap myself to wake up. 'Trudy, girl,' I say. 'You better watch out or the same thing's gonna happen to you that happened to Gladys Farnsworth last week.' Someone broke in and stole her TV and electric blanket and Lord knows what all. Like to have cleaned her out and her asleep in her bed the whole time. It's hard to say what would've happened if she'd been younger and better looking. I don't know what I'd do if I was to wake up and find a man in the house with me." She pauses to catch her breath. "How long can you stay?"

"Not long," Earl tells her. "I was just out this way and thought I'd stop in a minute."

"You can stay longer than that. I know you can. You haven't been out here for at least three weeks. I got some frozen dinners. I'll put a couple in the oven, and we can talk."

"I bought a chicken. We could fix it. Have mashed potatoes and the works just like Mom used to."

"I got some good spaghetti dinners. With lots of meat-balls," Trudy says, heading toward the kitchen.

Earl follows and sits on a stool beside the stove. The kitchen hasn't changed much since he was a boy except that it's cleaner and less busy. The only thing new is a microwave on the counter.

"A present," Trudy says. "From me to me." She winks. "You live alone long enough, you learn to treat yourself. The man at Big Lots says these things are safe. He bought one last Christmas for his son. Lucy at the library told me she read where microwaves can give you cancer up to twenty feet." Trudy shrugs. "Who knows what to believe. We've all got to go sometime. I'd a whole lot rather be killed by a microwave as by a man in my house." She takes a package from the freezer while holding back an avalanche of TV dinners with her other hand. "Have some spaghetti with me."

Earl shakes his head. In all the years he lived here, he never saw his mother fix a meal that wasn't made from scratch.

"Come here a minute," Trudy says. "I want you to see how this thing works." She opens the microwave door, pops her dinner in the tiny oven, and punches some buttons. "That's all there is to it. Isn't it one of the cleverest gadgets you ever saw?" She peeks through the microwave window and smiles.

"It's Friday night," Earl says. "You ought to be out doing something."

Trudy looks at him with genuine surprise. "I am doing something. I'm fixing supper and talking to you." She bends her knees and moves her face a little closer to the window.

"I'd just give anything to know what goes on in there, but I'm afraid to get too close to the thing after what Lucy said."

"I want to talk," says Earl.

"Good," says Trudy. "Let's talk." She moves her hand around the outside of the microwave like a magician showing an audience there are no trick wires. She shakes her head. "You'd think there'd at least be some heat."

Earl shifts his weight from one leg to the other and looks around the kitchen. "I think there's something wrong with me," he says.

Trudy looks alarmed. "Where?"

Earl shakes his head. "Not like that. I mean wrong like I'm missing something. You know? Then other times I think I'm the only one who's not."

Trudy relaxes. She chews on a fingernail, then holds her hand out to inspect the damage.

"And then there are times when I think no one's missing a damn thing. Maybe there just isn't any more," Earl says.

The buzzer goes off. Trudy sets her dinner on the table. "Are you sure you won't eat with me?"

"I'm sure," Earl says.

She begins to cut up meatballs. "I know what you mean. I miss being married. People say you don't miss what you've never had." She shakes her fork at Earl. "That's a bunch of baloney. You remember that man who came here once with Uncle Rymer? The one who had lost some fingers?" She takes a bite and signals for Earl to wait a minute while she chews. "Doesn't matter. You were little. Anyway, this man had lost his fingers. Lawn mower, I think. I remember him sitting here in the kitchen one night telling Mom and me how much he missed those fingers. He said he could still feel them even though they weren't there anymore. We thought he was the biggest liar we'd ever heard. Now I'm not so sure. I think a person can miss a part of himself even if it's *never* been there." Trudy frowns as though she has confused herself.

"Being married isn't everything," Earl says.

"It is if you've never been married." Trudy stares at Earl a moment, then leans across the table. "I want to tell you something. The strangest thing," she says, whispering. "I was at the library the other day, and I saw this book. The title just jumped out and grabbed me like a hand around my throat. *How to Make a Man Fall in Love with You.* That's what it said. I'll admit I was tempted, and I stood there a good long while. I knew if I stood there long enough, I'd pick that book up, so I just left. 'Trudy, girl,' I said, 'there's not a thing in this world wrong with you. You're fine just the way you are, and it's not your fault men can't see that.' "

Earl reaches for Trudy's hand, but she moves it.

"I believe in marriage," she says fiercely. "I got to believe in something."

Earl nods.

"Listen to me," she says. "You're not missing a thing. You've got it all, and you've got it good. And whatever you've got that's less than good is a whole lot better than nothing. Take it from one who knows."

Trudy finishes her spaghetti and carries her pan to the sink. She wipes her eyes on a dishtowel. "Law!" she exclaims brightly. She holds up the chicken and looks at Earl. "Who put this thing in here? You shoulda said something about this, Earl, honey. Has it been laying out the whole time you were here? It'll rot on you if you aren't careful." She gives the chicken to Earl.

As Trudy walks Earl to the car, she talks about the weather. "Cheer up," she says. "It's spring. And don't stay away so long next time. It gets pretty lonesome out here."

"Come over," Earl says. He gets into the car.

"What's that?" She points to the red spot on the seat.

"Chicken blood."

Trudy curls her lip and laughs. "Looks like it died there."

"It did," Earl says and drives away.

On his way home, he stops at the Chicken Coop, home of Ruth's famous Crispy Fried. A group of high school kids lounge on the hoods of their souped-up cars in the parking lot. "TGIF" they have written on the sides and dusty rear windows. Hearing their laughter, Earl suddenly feels like he's in a foreign country and cannot speak the language. He knows what the letters mean. What he's forgotten is the feeling that made him want to write them in the first place.

Inside, a dark-haired woman with oily skin stands behind the counter. She looks like she's eaten livers and gizzards every day of her life.

While Earl waits in line, he rattles the change in his pockets and looks around the room. Men, his age and older, all without their wives, seem to be waiting for something, too. They look like they're not sure whether it's something that hasn't happened or something that already has and somehow passed them by. Chuckie Wright, Neal Page, Alan Donovan—all graduates of Farlanburg High. They have more in common tonight than diplomas and chicken, Earl knows.

Near the door, Louie Taylor sits by himself, smoking and staring out the window. He graduated the same year as Earl; he was captain of the basketball team. He has the face of a man who's only recently begun to appreciate what he has lost. Now he drives for Hallawell and jokes around town that if hauling chemicals doesn't kill him, living with his wife, Connie, will.

Earl rattles the change in his pockets so loudly now that a

couple of men in line in front of him turn to look. Suddenly, he's very hungry and mad about having to wait. He heads for the door. Louie flashes a big-toothed grin and grabs him by the arm.

"How's it going, Earl ole buddy?" he says. "Doing the town tonight?"

Earl forces a smile. "On my way home," he says. He looks at the pile of bones on Louie's tray.

"I'm going to quit eating here because of these deformed chickens," Louie says. "Damned things don't have no legs or thighs. Nothing but backs and wings." He laughs loudly and rubs his balding head.

"My mother made a helluva fried chicken," Earl says.

"No kidding," says Louie. "Mine, too. When you figure out how they did it, let me know, will you? Seems either one of us could do a sight better than this."

At home, Earl pulls in the driveway, shuts off the motor, and leans his head back against the seat. The curtains in the house are closed, but he has a clear picture of what's waiting for him inside.

He opens the car door, picks up the chicken, and gets out. The smell of steak is everywhere. Inside, he walks down the hallway, leaving a trail of blood behind him on the rug. The mister is sacked out in the recliner in the living room, his hand loosely holding the remote-control box for the TV. His mouth is open, ready to receive any leftovers that might come his way while he sleeps.

Mary's lying on the couch, eyes closed, hands together under her cheek. It's hard to tell whether she's sleeping or praying.

Earl can hear Kim and Kerry giggling in their room. Brenda

and the missus do dishes. Glasses, plates, forks, and spoons. Brenda methodically washes and plunges them into the water to rinse. She holds her lips together tightly as if she's afraid something inside her might rupture if she spoke.

Mrs. Kivett dries. When she sees Earl standing in the doorway, she opens her mouth but doesn't say anything. She's spent a lifetime not saying anything, and she's proud of it. She can't stand the sight of the mister, but she can honestly say they've never had a fight.

Brenda looks up. She spies the pool of blood from the chicken forming on the linoleum. "What are you doing?" she shrieks.

The missus looks at the paper towels but doesn't move. Her hand flutters nervously about her throat.

Earl throws the chicken on the kitchen table and starts toward his and Brenda's room. As he passes through the living room again, he glances at Mary, who has opened her eyes and is watching him. Her jaw drops for what he thinks will be a yawn, then ever so slowly she closes and reopens one eye. Mary smiles her secret smile. Today, she is wearing green anklets. She knows what it takes to be happy.

Earl stares at her for a moment, then looks at the floor. He returns to the kitchen, takes a bottle of oil from the refrigerator, then opens the bottom drawer of the stove.

Brenda starts to say something, but she shuts up as Earl turns around with a cast-iron skillet in his hand. He raises the skillet in the air. The missus whimpers.

"We have a problem," he says, as he turns the skillet over and dumps rat droppings onto the floor. He sets the skillet on the stove. To fry good chicken you have to boil your bird before you ever put it in the frying pan, his mother used to say. Earl doesn't have a recipe for chicken, and his chicken won't be as good as his mother's. But he smiles as he goes about his work. Frying chicken is not the only thing he'll have to talk himself into, he knows, but he figures it's as good a place as any to start.

when Della called the parsonage. Mary Sue was practicing church hymns on her old-fashioned organ, and she continued to play while she talked. Della could hear her chording.

"He's a professor at Oklahoma State," Della said. "He has tenure." She had never really understood what tenure meant, but it seemed important to Frank because he always mentioned it, so when someone struck up a conversation about her son and inquired as to the nature of his employment, Della did what Frank did and casually tossed it in.

"A professor!" said Mary Sue. "Imagine! You just bring him right along with you. We'll find something for him to do."

"I can't ask him to do that," said Della. "It's his vacation."

There was a slight pause in the music as though the organ had hiccupped or someone had turned a page. "Come alone then," said Mary Sue. "You'll be down here and back each morning before they even miss you."

Della considered it. "You're probably right, but I want to spend lots of time with my grandson. You know kids: 'Grandma, will you take me fishing? Grandma, will you take me berry picking?' I thought we'd all go over to Pritchett State Park for a picnic one afternoon. It's a long way over there. We'll be gone most of the day."

"You'll have plenty of time," said Mary Sue. "You can leave right after you finish here and still get over there and back. You don't want to go too early anyway. It's cold up in those mountains until noon. Besides, if you cancel out on me, who's gonna teach your class? No one could do as good a job as you."

Mary Sue was in charge of the senior-high class. She requested them. "I'm a natural with teenagers," she often said. "It's amazing the influence the right teacher can have in just one week."

Extended
Learning

Della Sayer had promised
Vacation Bible School the first through the fifth of Au⟩
when Frank phoned to say he and his family would be
for a visit that same week, Della regretted her prom
decided to wiggle out of it. It wasn't that she didn't
help her class make macaroni sculptures or pop-up j
Frank was her son, her only child, and he hadn't been
two years. He was married to a dentist named Mar
quiet, fragile-wristed woman with lovely teeth. Della
forward to spending time with her son and his wife, bu
her grandson, eight-year-old T. Barry, she really wa⟩
see.

She knew God would understand her predicamer
wasn't sure about the pastor's wife, a tightly perme
woman named Mary Sue.

"Frank's living out west now, isn't he?" said Mar⟩

Della had the preschoolers. She taught them every year, though she doubted how much they got out of it. Ask them two weeks later what they remembered about Bible school, and nine times out of ten, they'd lick their lips and say, "Cookies." She often thought it might be just as effective and a whole lot cleaner to give them each a bag of Oreos and turn them loose outside where they could climb trees or roll in the grass and get on with the business of appreciating the world God had given them.

"I'm really sorry," said Della, "but you're going to have to find someone else. You've got plenty of time. You won't have any problem."

The music picked up a new sound, and Della guessed she was hearing a little touch of bass. "Let's be honest," said Mary Sue. "Can we? We've all got other things we'd rather do. There are fifty-two weeks in the year, and we're talking about one of them. Ten to fifteen hours total. Is that too much for the Lord?"

"I explained the whole thing to Him last night," said Della. "He didn't seem to think there was any problem."

The organ suddenly sounded as if someone had pulled out all the stops and floored the swell pedal. "Be that way," said Mary Sue.

Della threw herself into a fit of cleaning and preparation. "Don't go to any trouble," Frank said, and Della assured him she wouldn't. She papered rooms and painted porches, baked and froze rhubarb cake and gooseberry pie, carried woods dirt to revitalize her flowers, and conned a telephone repairman into helping her rig up a tire swing in the sycamore tree at the lower end of her yard.

"It's for my grandson," Della explained.

The repairman winked. "That's what they all say," he replied.

Della lived alone on a farm seven miles south of Farlanburg. It wasn't a farm in the working sense, but there were enough cows to keep the weeds down, and, at last count, a dozen chickens that occasionally scratched up enough energy to drop an egg in the grass. The nearest neighbors, the Peevys, lived more than a mile away, which meant Della could hoe her garden in her nightgown if she wanted, and when she felt the urge to get out her gasoline can and set fire to a pile of brush, there was no one whose permission she had to ask.

During the summer, she took her bath when evening first began to trickle into the hollow, then she would sit out on her back porch and revel in the beauty of her flowers and the smell of her own clean skin. She liked to watch the shadows creep up the hills, over rock and fence and thicket, climbing higher, covering ridge tops, until her world was submerged in darkness and the moon looked like the sun seen from the bottom of a clear blue lake. At the same time each night, if the dogs behaved themselves and didn't start their infernal yapping, a whippoorwill would slip out of the woods and sing on a hillside rock. Della would yawn and think her farm a dandy place to live and the best place in the world to visit, and she would climb the stairs to bed surprised she didn't have company more often.

Common sense told her the best part of her life was behind her and she ought to be depressed, but Royce had always said she was low on common sense, which explained, she supposed, why she woke most mornings feeling happy. Royce was her husband, dead now almost ten years. He was a big, florid-faced man who lived to eat, and when he wasn't eating, he worked at his sawmill. He was on his way to town one

Saturday morning to get a haircut when the Volkswagen he was driving was hit head-on by a coal truck. The accident happened in the curve near the Pullman Creek Methodist church, and a woman named Oma Dalton was mowing the church cemetery at the time. She called Della. "They's a man dead over here, tore all to hell!" Oma shouted into the phone. "I don't know who he is, but a bunch of people standin' around down by the highway gave me your name and said I ought to call you."

Della was reluctant at the funeral to believe that the waxy, rouged thing in the casket had ever been Royce, but the weekly newspaper confirmed it: "Rescue Squad Uses 'Jaws of Life' to Extract Local Man from Car." The article featured pictures of the death car, or what was left of it, and though the pictures were in black and white, Della knew the real color of the dark spot that covered most of the front seat.

"In this life, you can never count on nothing," Royce was fond of saying, and the suddenness of his departure seemed to bear that out. Even in death, he had a sly, knowing look on his face as if to say, "See. Told you I was right."

Frank and his family arrived on a Sunday night, exhausted from being on the road two days. They pulled their Volvo into Della's barn lot a little after ten o'clock and left a white trail of Styrofoam cups and empty food containers behind them as they lugged suitcases and pillows through the dewy, moonlit yard. Della met them on the porch, arms open wide. "Frank!" she said. "Son!"

"Hello, Mom," said Frank. He was a tall man with thinning hair and poor posture. He had a well-trimmed beard, a Ph.D. from Purdue University, and had been a forestry professor at OSU for the past eleven years. In photographs taken of him during professional meetings or departmental wingdings, he appeared bright-eyed and very distinguished, Della thought. But the Frank who came to her house always arrived bleary-eyed, with bugs on his windshield, and he acted as if some essential part of himself had been overlooked in the packing and left behind.

Della kissed her son and hugged him tightly, then turned and embraced Marjorie, who had lifted her foot and was frowning at something on the bottom of her left shoe.

"What is it?" asked Della, and Marjorie showed her.

"Ornery dogs," Della said. "Sorry about that."

While Frank headed back to the car for more suitcases, Marjorie stepped off the porch and wiped her sandal in the grass. She was thin and blonde, in her early forties, and the liveliest thing about her was her green pedal pushers and flowered blouse. When Frank first brought her home, Marjorie was still in dental school, and Della had been amazed that any person, especially one so young, could be so serene. She had kidded Frank on the phone and had written letters reminding him of the old saying: still water runs deep. But after fifteen years of observing her daughter-in-law, Della had amended the saying to create a new version which seemed more accurate: still water doesn't run at all.

Frank returned with more suitcases, and he handed Snapper, their new dog, to Marjorie.

"Where's T. Barry?" Della asked.

"Asleep," said Frank. "I'll get him."

Della was disappointed but tried not to show it. She turned her attention to Snapper, who was struggling frantically in Marjorie's arms. "Hello, Snapper," she said. "Are you tired, too?" He was a small, kinky-haired dog with stains below his eyes that made him look as if he'd been crying mud. He belonged to a professor in Frank's department, but the man and his family had gone overseas on sabbatical, so Frank and Marjorie had agreed to keep him awhile.

"What kind of dog is it? You said on the phone, but I forgot."

"A peekapoo," said Marjorie. "He's a cross between a Pekingese and a poodle."

"Funny-looking thing," said Della. "I think he wants down."

Marjorie continued to hold him. "He's house-trained. He thinks he's human."

"Poor peekaboo," said Della, petting his head. "My dogs aren't here. They're out courting. Put him down and let him run loose, why don't you?"

As soon as his paws touched ground, Snapper lifted his leg and hiked on Della's marigolds. When he finished, he began to explore the yard with quick, greedy sniffs.

"Look at him go!" said Della.

"I'd better get him. He'll be filthy," said Marjorie.

Frank returned with three more suitcases, one in each hand and an overnight case under his arm.

"Is he awake, yet?" Della asked. "I can't wait any longer. Let me get him." She pulled her sweater around her and started out the walk, but Frank stopped her.

"I'll get him, Mom. He's sound asleep. You'll have plenty of time to spend with him tomorrow."

Della could count on one hand the number of times she had seen her grandson. She often wondered if she would even recognize him if she met him on the street. She knew that before the age of ten, two years can make a big change in a life. "You need to bring the boy out here to see me more often," she said every time she called Frank.

"Road runs two ways," he reminded her.

He was right, Della knew, but the older she got, the less she liked to travel. How could she tell her son, who had half his life ahead of him, that although she was in good health and not afraid of dying, she didn't want to do it in a strange bed, several hundred miles from home?

It bothered her to have a grandchild she didn't know. She had known both sets of her grandparents and thought herself a better person because of it. Such was life these days, she supposed; have children and you cast a part of yourself to the wind. She was grateful to know where the seeds had landed. Was it asking so much to want to watch them grow?

She talked to T. Barry on the phone every couple of weeks, but it was hard to tell much about a person when you asked, "What're you doing?" and he said, "Talking to you." He was going to be whatever he was going to be, Della knew, but whatever that was, he hadn't turned into it yet, and in the limited time she was allowed to spend with him, she hoped to have some sort of impact on his life, though exactly what sort of impact she hoped to have was still vague in her mind. It was a selfish, conceited notion, she reckoned, but there were things she wanted to teach him, such as how to be happy by learning to appreciate the little things in life: sitting under a tin roof during a warm summer rain, eating persimmons after the first frost, building a hay house in a barn in winter, or watching bees emerge from the hive on the first warm days of March. She wanted to teach him how to avoid the ho-hums, the blahs, and the wearies, that crafty trio that played tricks on a person by appearing years away when really they were not. "Come down off your high horse," she could almost hear Royce saying, and if he'd been there he would have teased her and made her feel starry-eyed and foolish and said something like, "Here you go. Trying to put up detour signs before the bridges are even washed out."

As Frank carried T. Barry through the yard, Della was surprised and a little sad to see how much he'd grown. She planted a kiss on his smooth cheek and held the door open for Frank. "I've fixed a place in your old room. I'll help you tuck him in."

"I wish you wouldn't," whispered Frank. "If he wakes up and sees you, he'll know he's not at home, and I'll never be able to get him back to sleep."

Gently, Della picked up her grandson's bare foot and kissed it, then she stood aside and let them pass. Frank took T. Barry upstairs while Marjorie roamed the yard calling "H-e-e-r-e Snapper, h-e-e-r-e Snapper." Della got a flashlight and helped her look. They finally found him out back in the weeds where Della burned trash.

"Ooooh, stinkie doggie," said Marjorie. She picked him up and swatted his rump.

"He's all right," said Della. "Just got a little soot on him. He's fine."

They took him inside, to the bathroom, and Della helped Marjorie clean off his paws. The dog lay on the edge of the sink, his body limp with resignation. He closed his eyes and assumed an expression Della had seen on the faces of women receiving a manicure.

"My dogs wouldn't hold still for this a minute," Della said.

"It's bred into house dogs," said Marjorie.

Della watched as Marjorie toweled him. "You must be worn out, too," she said. "Let me fix you something to eat. I've got butterscotch pies in the warming oven and a pot of hot coffee on the stove."

Marjorie put her hand over her mouth to stifle a yawn, then

checked her watch. "Thanks," she said, "but we never eat after six o'clock."

Della carried the suitcases into the downstairs guest bedroom, unable to shake the feeling she was giving shelter to tourists. While Marjorie unpacked and settled Snapper in his basket, Della headed for the kitchen. She had no rules about when she ate; she ate whenever she was hungry—a bad habit, she supposed, probably bred into her. As she passed through the dining room, she was about to close the inside door that led onto the back porch, but she stopped, surprised to see Frank out there in the dark. The screen door was covered with bugs and moths and millers, beating delicate wings against the mesh. Frank stood, arms folded, leaning against the porch post, and Della was struck by an almost uncontrollable urge to slip out there and scratch his back. She put her hand on the screen door but withdrew it because it occurred to her that he might have gone out there to be alone. What was it like, she wondered, to come home after two years? Did home still *feel* like home, was it a place you were instinctively drawn to, or did you come because you thought you ought to, because the navigator in you happened to remember the way?

       At eleven o'clock the next morning, Frank and Marjorie were still asleep. The sun had completed half its arc across the sky, and Della's dogs, two male mongrels, had already lumbered off to find shade. Silvervine, the cat, just returned from hunting, sat licking her paws and sunning herself on the walk.

Della had been up since five. When she was younger, she used to crave sleep. She dreamed of going to bed before dark and nesting there until noon the next day, but now that she had the opportunity, she had lost the inclination, which was just as well, she supposed, considering she had a grandson to attend to and a turn of light bread to make.

T. Barry sat beside her on the back porch steps, hands on his knees, a wrinkled bag full of hickory nuts in his lap. Della had gathered the nuts last fall from the big shagbarks that lined the road below her house and had stored them in a box on the top shelf of her cupboard until the insides were sweet and chewy, the shells the color of clean sand. She had saved them for this occasion, and at the end of the week, she planned to send what was left home with T. Barry with the hope that each time he cracked one, he'd remember the fun they'd had. She scooped a handful from the bag, tapped one with her hammer, then dropped the kernel into her grandson's open mouth. "So," she said. "Tell me again what the T. stands for. It's Timothy or Terrence or Tutwyler. My memory's not as good as it used to be, you understand."

The boy chewed steadily and looked at Della out of clear, deep-set gray eyes. He was a quiet kid with thick, blond hair cut so his head appeared peanut-shaped and difficult to balance. His arms and legs were remarkably unscarred and new looking, as though he hadn't figured out what to do with himself from the neck down. "It stands for Thurman," he said, shyly. "You know that."

Della nodded and cracked another nut, this time for herself. "Maybe," she said, "and maybe I just wanted to see if *you* did. I knew a man once, a pitiful fellow, who got kicked in the head by a horse and couldn't remember his own name. He went crazy trying to remember it, so they locked him in a corncrib and kept him there till he died."

T. Barry frowned and studied Della's crib. The rock supports at the two front corners had crumbled during the years, allowing the north side of the building to sit down, but the south side was still stable and several feet off the ground. Della liked her corncrib, though she had to admit it was hazardous. It reminded her of the hotrods the young boys drove through town.

"I don't believe that," said T. Barry. "It's against the law to lock someone in a corncrib."

"They abolished that law," said Della. "I guess you're not familiar with the Corncrib Act."

Behind them, inside the kitchen, Snapper whined and dug at the screen. Della had walked him earlier and would have let him out to run in the yard, but Marjorie had forbidden it. "Not as long as your dogs are home," she'd said. "Fleas."

T. Barry bit down hard on an unshelled nut. "What's 'abolish'?"

"It means to do away with, to get rid of. Don't worry about it though. I still think you're plenty smart."

"I'm in the E.L.P."

"Sorry," said Della. "I didn't know." She tilted her head and looked at her grandson through her bifocals. "What's the E.L.P.?"

"Extended Learning Program. It's a thing for smart kids at my school."

"Oh," said Della. "Are you smart?"

T. Barry shrugged. "They say I am."

"They say a lot of things," said Della.

"I'm smart enough not to believe everything you tell me. Mama and Daddy say you have a bad habit of making things up."

Della laughed. "I don't know why grown-ups do that."

"Do what?"

"Try to keep things from kids." Della shook her head. "Fifty cents says they'll tell you there's no such thing as the Corncrib Act."

"I'll ask them," said T. Barry, rising.

"Go ahead. I guess I'd better hurry inside and fix their breakfast. But I must say I was having fun sitting out here cracking nuts and talking to you."

T. Barry rolled a nut with the toe of his shoe, then sat down again. "Is it true about that crazy man? I want you to tell me the truth."

"Of course it is," said Della.

"Tell me his name, then."

"Can't do that."

"Why not?"

"If he didn't know it, how do you expect me to?"

The day turned out to be a scorcher. By three o'clock that afternoon, the temperature had reached the mid-nineties, and the cows had wandered off the hills and stood under the apple trees below the house, chewing cuds and flicking matted tails at the flies.

Della's house had no air-conditioning, but she kept fans in most of the windows. On humid days, the only really cool spot on the place was the cellar because it was partially under the hill, and occasionally, Della would pull a chair in there and relax or take a flashlight and admire the variety of colors in her canned fruits and vegetables. Earlier, she had mentioned the cellar to Frank and Marjorie, but neither of them took her up on it, so she assumed they weren't too uncomfortable with the heat. She had also suggested they all get in her car and go for a drive to enjoy the countryside, maybe get an ice cream cone, her treat, but no one had seemed especially wild about that idea.

"Don't think you have to entertain us," said Frank. "You just go on and do your thing, and so will we, and that way we can all relax."

"I *am* relaxed," said Della. "I just thought you might enjoy getting out and seeing the sights."

"I grew up around here, Mom. Remember?"

"Things change," said Della. "You've been gone a long time."

Della stood in her kitchen, rolling and cutting egg noodles. She had the radio on to help pass the time. Frank was asleep, Marjorie was reading, and T. Barry lay stretched out on the living room floor doing his homework. It was their first full day of vacation, and Della wanted it to be memorable and exciting.

"Homework?" she had said when Marjorie told T. Barry it was time to get his books. "It's summer."

"He takes a test in three weeks when school starts. He has to have a high score if he wants to stay in the E.L.P. That's a program for gifted kids at his school."

Della looked at her daughter-in-law over the top of her glasses.

"He enjoys it," said Marjorie. "At home, he'd much rather be inside reading or fooling with his computer than outside with the other kids playing in the street."

"You think that's normal?"

"What's normal?" said Marjorie.

"Homework," Della said to herself as she picked up a big knife and sliced off sections from the roll of noodle dough. Frank had never done homework during the summer, and as far as school went, he had certainly done all right.

At the moment, he was snoring in the front porch swing. He had eaten his breakfast a little after noon and had gone upstairs and prowled through some boxes of old books. He was asleep again when Della went to check on him at two. The noodles were for him; Della hoped they might enliven him. When he was a boy, his favorite dish had been a concoction of homemade egg noodles and beans. In those days, he liked to fish and hunt, and he spent hours walking the creek banks or just wandering over the hills. Back then, he'd come home with burrs in his socks and a craving for noodles, and Della had wound up fixing them once or twice a week. Now, he insisted they weren't worth the trouble it took to make them. Della loved her son dearly and was proud of his accomplishments, but there were moments when she was struck by the unmotherly thought that, at some point, he had turned into one of the most boring people she knew.

He had done well in high school and had earned a scholarship to the state university. Four years had turned into six, six into ten; more than half his life had been spent in school. He had knocked off all the rough edges, but in the process, something else had been knocked off, too. Though he could tell her there was a statistically significant correlation between canopy tree mortality and drought-induced stress, he could not tell her how to save her wild chestnut trees. And Della was surprised and, secretly, a little disappointed the first time she discovered that, unlike his father, he could not recognize a white oak suitable for veneer from one destined for crossties.

Neither she nor Royce had any education beyond high school, and Royce had always been proud that his son was smart and had done so well at books. "It's the way the world's goin'," he had said when Frank finished his Ph.D. "Gettin' an education is the ticket to a better life." There was a slightly wistful tone to his voice that Della hadn't heard before.

"Oh, I don't know about that," she said. "I don't have an education, and I'm happy with my life." She laughed. "Why, I don't know as I could stand it if it got any better."

Royce smiled, patted her shoulder, and said, "Some are

just easier satisfied than others," which caused Della to wonder for weeks whether he knew something about their life that she didn't.

Della lifted the noodle sections, combing with her fingers until the yellow strips unwound and lay like a pile of shorn curls. Through the kitchen window, she had a clear view of Marjorie, who was stretched out in a lawn chair in the backyard. She was a good visitor, really, no more trouble than the cows. She did not hang around the kitchen and get in the way by trying to be useful, nor did she rattle on about the food and interrupt Della's work by asking for recipes. All she wanted was to be left alone with her book, and occasionally, she would look up and inquire whether there was any iced tea.

She was Frank's wife, and Della wanted to like her, but Frank's wife or not, she wasn't very lively, and Della often wondered how she worked up enough energy to pull a tooth. Della recalled having a tooth pulled by a dentist, a Dr. Weeble, when she was a child, and what she remembered most about the experience was not the pain or the blood but the look on Dr. Weeble's face as he rolled up his sleeves, rubbed his hands together, and told her to say, "Aaahhh." It was an eager, alive look, one that said, "I am *passionate* about teeth!" To be good at anything, you had to feel passionate about it, Della had always believed, the way she felt about the people she loved, the way Royce had felt about trees.

"If you had only ten minutes left on earth, how would you spend them?" she once asked Royce, and, without hesitation, he told her he'd go to the woods, lie on his back, and look at trees. At the time, she was hurt because he hadn't said he'd spend his last moments with her. Looking back on it, she thought she recognized a rare, uncalculating honesty and a genuine love of nature in his answer, and she wished he were around to instill a little of that love in their grandson.

When she had finished with the noodles, Della washed her hands and tip-toed into the living room. T. Barry lay on his stomach, studying. Seeing him like that took Della back almost thirty years. He looked so much like Frank from certain angles.

"Psstt," she said.

He glanced up.

"You don't look like you're having much fun," she said. "Are you having fun at Grandma Della's house?"

He wrinkled his nose. "You've got something awful in your carpet," he said, pointing at a dark spot in the pile.

Della knelt and examined it. "That's not something awful," she said. "It's a mashed raisin. Your better brand of carpets come that way."

T. Barry looked skeptical.

"It's true," said Della. "The manufacturers put little pieces of food in there so the people who buy the carpets will have something to fall back on in case of hard times."

T. Barry put his face closer to the raisin and peered at it. "You're making that up," he said. "I bet it doesn't say that in any carpet books."

"Just because it's not written down somewhere doesn't mean it's not true. Grandma Della loves T. Barry. True or false?"

He shrugged. "True."

"See," said Della. "You believe that without reading it." She untied her apron and took it off. "Are you finished with your homework?"

He shook his head.

"Too bad. I was looking for someone to take a walk with me."

"I've got to do my math," said T. Barry.

Della picked at the raisin. "What's nine plus nine?"

He rolled his eyes and looked insulted. "That's easy. Eighteen."

Della held up her hand. "Ding-a-ling-a-ling."

"What's that?"

"A bell," she said. "School's out. You already know more than me."

Della had carefully planned the week. There was so much to do while Frank was home and so little time to do it. On Tuesday evening, she wanted to have a wiener roast, and she had invited the neighbor children, the Peevys. But when she asked Frank to gather wood and cut sticks, she discovered that neither he nor Marjorie nor T. Barry ate wieners anymore because they were leery of the ingredients added to the meat.

Frank pulled a package out of the refrigerator and pointed to the fine print on the label. "Look at this. Sodium nitrite, all kinds of additives. You don't want to eat that stuff, Mom. Don't you know what it can do to you?"

Della listened and shook her head in pretend dismay while Frank went on about the general laxity of the Food and Drug Administration. She waited until he had finished his spiel. "Will you all eat chicken?" she asked.

The five Peevy children showed up at six o'clock, barefooted, carrying a half-empty bag of marshmallows. Della had forgotten to call them to tell them not to come. They sat in the dusty road in front of the house. Della was trying to get supper on the table, and she wouldn't have known they were out there if Snapper, who was locked on the front porch, hadn't barked and scratched at the screen. The oldest boy, Bud, who was T. Barry's age, was standing in the yard when Della went out. He put his hands in his pockets and alternated between looking at the sky and his feet. "We come for the weenies," he said.

Della stretched her mouth into a smile and herded the children around back. She poured each a glass of Kool-Aid, then went back inside to get T. Barry to come out and play. He refused. He stood at the dining room door, hands on the screen, and looked at the Peevys as if he were the one on the outside observing caged animals at a zoo. Della switched the burner on her stove from medium to low so she wouldn't burn the chicken, dumped the mashed potatoes into the Crockpot to keep them hot, stuck the raisin pie in the warming oven, then took off her apron and went outside to entertain her guests.

For the first fifteen minutes, they sipped their drinks and told Della what all they had been doing, and when they grew restless, she let them chase her cat. After a short time, the cat grew tired and so did they, and it became clear to everyone that the fun had peaked.

Bud stood, hands in his pockets, and blushed. "We got to go now," he said. "But I want to thank you for invitin' us."

Della had always admired politeness and guests who knew when to leave. "You are more than welcome," she said. "We'll have to get together and do it again sometime."

Bud rounded up his brothers and sisters and made them say thank you, and Della gave them two packs of wieners and buns and sent them on their way.

Early Wednesday morning, before anyone else was up, Della's brother Harve called to ask if Frank and his family had made it home. Della told him they'd arrived on

Sunday night, but as soon as she said it, she began to have doubts because it seemed they'd already been there at least a week.

"I hope it was a good trip," said Harve, and Della said it was.

"No close calls, I suppose. No wrecks or anything like that."

"Not that I know of," said Della.

"That's good," said Harve, "but they still have to worry about getting back. Most people get killed within twenty-five miles of home."

Della sighed. "Is that a fact?"

"It sure is," said Harve, and he tried to remember when and where he'd read it. "Getting around to the reason I called," he said. "I wanted to invite you all out to our place this evening for supper. Doris is making a red velvet cake, and Elaine and her kids are coming out. Nothing fancy. Just a little get-together."

Della wanted to know what she could bring and Harve said nothing, and Della said she couldn't just come and eat, and Harve said, all right. "Whip up a gallon of potato salad and stop by the Piggly Wiggly for hamburger," he said. "And if you happen to have some extra charcoal, bring it along. You can help me fire up the grill."

At breakfast that morning, Frank announced that he and Marjorie planned to drive up to the mall in Clendenin to see the new Jack Nicholson movie, and that they wouldn't be back in time. "Seems silly to have to drive to another county to see a movie," said Frank, and Marjorie agreed. "What you need is a theater in Farlanburg," he said. "It'd give some of those kids you see hanging out at the pool hall something to do."

Della was fixing breakfast, and she was not interested in

the hoods at the pool hall. She dropped a hot blueberry waffle onto Frank's plate. "You don't want to waste your time watching a movie," she told him. "You can do that in Oklahoma." She had never been to Oklahoma, and before Frank went out there, she had envisioned it as a desert with nothing for miles but red dust. She had been surprised to discover that the state had a forestry department; the wasteland she had pictured did not include trees. At some point, she had added stores and a post office to her scene, and adding a theater seemed relatively easy compared to the initial adjustments she'd had to make. She put a large pat of butter on Frank's waffle and passed him the syrup. "You've always liked Uncle Harve and Aunt Doris. They'll be disappointed if they don't get to see you."

"They know where I live," said Frank.

T. Barry was still upstairs asleep, and Della was glad because she didn't want him to get the impression that Jack Nicholson movies were anywhere near as interesting or important as a trip to Uncle Harve's farm. She poured another cup of batter into the waffle iron, then turned to Marjorie, who was breaking off bits of sausage and dropping them under the table. "T. Barry would have a such a good time," she said. "He'd get to pet pigs and ride ponies. When does he get a chance to have an experience like that?"

Marjorie wiped her hands on her napkin and looked at Frank. "Not very often," she said, "if he can help it. He's not really the outdoorsy type."

Della broke off a piece of unclaimed waffle and ate it. She threw an equally large piece under the table, which prompted a chain of events that began with toenail action on the linoleum and ended with a teeny-weeny growl. "Don't you want him to appreciate nature?" Della asked.

"He does. We all do. But that doesn't mean we want to wallow in it," said Frank.

Della would have liked to continue the discussion, but she decided not to because she didn't want the day to get off to a bad start. She did, however, risk mentioning the fact that T. Barry might enjoy playing with some other kids. "Elaine and her boys will be there. It would be good for T. Barry to run and romp with them."

"He doesn't particularly like Elaine's boys," said Frank. "Last time we were home, the big one, what's his name, hit him in the head with a rock. Remember?"

"That was probably Roger," Della said. "He's in 4-H camp this week. He won't even be there."

"Neither will we," said Frank.

Della planned to take T. Barry out to Harve and Doris's farm whether Frank and Marjorie went or not, but in the end, she changed her mind. T. Barry didn't seem all that keen on going. She called Harve and apologized and said that Frank was run ragged trying to visit everybody, but that he'd be sure to stop by and see them before he went back.

Frank and Marjorie went to Clendenin to see the Jack Nicholson movie, and Della and T. Barry sat in the living room listening to the metronomic ticking of the clock. "What do we want to do?" she asked him, and he said it didn't matter.

"Of course it does," said Della. "Everything matters," but even as she said it, she had doubts. They sat, side by side, on Della's lumpy couch. "Help me think," she said. "I'll take you fishing, I'll play ball with you, we can go hiking, we can—"

"Watch cartoons," said T. Barry. He got up and flipped on the TV set.

"What's on?" asked Della.

" 'Teenage Mutant Ninja Turtles,' " he said.

Della watched about five minutes, then got her sun hat from the hook behind the kitchen door and followed the path to the garden. She pulled a few weeds from around the tomatoes and checked the cabbage heads for worms. When she finished, she sat down on the wooden stool she used for corn shucking. High overhead, a hawk circled, wobbling a little in flight. Della gazed at the green, wooded hills and at the creek she used to water her plants. She picked up a handful of dirt, letting the loose soil sift between her fingers. "Is this worth nothing?" she asked.

When she went to the house, T. Barry lay in the recliner, half asleep. "Wake up," Della said. "We're going on an adventure."

"I don't want to go on an adventure," he said. He yawned and turned on his side.

"You just think you don't," Della said, trying to rouse him with her cheerfulness. "We're going berry picking. I know a place back on the ridge where there are blackberries as big around as my finger."

T. Barry gripped both armrests and scowled.

Della tried to persuade him by promising to bake a cobbler and when that didn't work, she told him she'd take him to see a haunted house. "Help me a little," she said. "I'm just trying to make sure you have a good time."

"There's no such thing," said T. Barry.

"No such thing as a good time?"

"No such thing as a haunted house. I don't believe in ghosts."

"You might if you saw one," said Della, kindly.

"No one on this planet has ever seen a ghost," he informed her, "and that includes you."

"Seeing has nothing to do with it," Della argued. "The

biggest part of what I believe in, I can't see." She scooted a footstool beside the recliner and sat down. "Do you believe in bird lice?"

T. Barry nodded.

"I do, too," said Della. "My eyes are bad now, so I can't see them, but I don't doubt for one minute that they're there. Just like I believe in trolls and witches and elves."

T. Barry laughed. "No you don't." He suddenly frowned. "Do you?"

"I believe in dragons, dead Ed Sullivan, and leprechauns," said Della, "Santa Claus, Jesus Christ, and the Easter bunny. And I believe little boys are little boys until they are big boys and that if they don't run and have fun and climb trees while they can, it will be too late because they'll forget how."

"Think about it," said Della. She picked up his hand and kissed it, then hurried into the kitchen. She packed sandwiches, apples, and cookies in a metal bucket and filled a mason jar with ice water. Her Polaroid was the only thing she lacked, and she found it in the bottom drawer of the china closet.

When she returned to the living room, she switched off the TV and knelt beside the recliner. "Please," she said. "Come with me."

T. Barry hesitated for an instant. He shook his head.

Della winked. "I'll let you have the biggest berries."

"Berries stain my teeth."

"I'll take you to town for a milk shake."

T. Barry leaned over the edge of the chair and picked up a copy of *TV Guide*. "It's too far into town. I don't want to go on an adventure," he said.

Della looked at her grandson. He was already much older than she'd thought. She went to the hall closet to get her purse and returned with a five-dollar bill. "Do you believe in this?"

T. Barry stared at the money.

"Come with me," said Della, "and it's yours."

The dirt road above the house was narrow and followed the creek. When Della was younger, it was well-traveled, connecting two main county highways. But during the years, shorter connectors had sprung up, serving more families, and the road was now used mostly by young boys buzzing dirt bikes and subdivision escapees who needed a place to tear up their Jeeps.

Foot-high weeds ran mohawk-style up the middle between two dusty tracks. Della walked on the left side, carrying her metal bucket, its handle squeaking and clanking with each step. T. Barry followed. He was so quiet that Della stopped periodically to make sure he was still there. "Why don't you walk beside me?' she suggested, pointing to the right track. "That way I can see you. I don't see you often enough." She took the bill out of the bucket. Without a word, T. Barry switched to the right track. She handed him the berry bucket and took his picture.

As they walked, she pointed out various historical sights and places of interest. "This is where your dad caught his first fish," she informed him. "We had a cow die from eating hedge apples over there." At the first creek crossing, they turned left and hiked a short distance until they came to a pile of rotting boards and a sawdust heap at the edge of a field. "This was where your grandpa had his last sawmill," said Della. "He had a mill, an old diesel motor, and an edger he dragged around from spot to spot."

They saw several deer tracks, surprised a quail, and ate

their picnic on a mossy spot in the woods. It was almost six o'clock when they headed back. They had no berries, but Della's bucket carried more than a dozen snapshots, proof of the outdoor experience they had shared. The adventure had cost her almost nine dollars, not including the initial five, but she didn't regret the expense. He had waded, skipped rocks, and caught minnows, and she had an especially nice shot of him on a grapevine, looking, if not thrilled, at least pleasant, on his joyless ride through the air.

His last night on the farm, T. Barry was tired and went to bed early. Marjorie had almost finished her book, and she asked if anyone would mind if she went to her room to read. Della washed the supper dishes, then went out on the back porch to spend time with Frank. He stood, eyes closed, head cocked as though listening to something running the ridge tops, moving away from him, almost out of range. Della leaned her head against his shoulder.

"Do you hear it?" she asked.

"Hear what, Mom?"

"Whatever you're listening for. Whatever it is you drove all this way to hear."

"I came home to be with you," said Frank.

Without worrying whether he was too old for it, Della began to scratch his back. You're ruining him, she imagined herself saying, but she could not imagine what good it would do, so they stood, without talking, and watched darkness settle over the hills.

Frank, Marjorie, and T. Barry left at six the next morning. The night had drained away, and a heavy fog filled the hollow. Marjorie carried Snapper from the house to the car, and as she strolled down the walk, he twisted his head as if craving one last look at Della's yard. Della said goodbye to Marjorie while Frank returned to the house to get T. Barry.

"You'll have to come out and see us," said Marjorie.

Della nodded. She rearranged pillows and covers in the back seat.

"I mean it. We've got plenty of room, and we're gone all day. You'd have the whole house to yourself."

"Thanks," said Della. "I may."

T. Barry was asleep when Frank carried him out. Della tucked him in and kissed his cheek. "There's a paper bag that belongs to him in the trunk," she whispered to Frank. He looked puzzled. "Hickory nuts," said Della. "Don't throw them away."

Della hugged her son and over his shoulder, she saw a bright patch of sun burning through the fog. "Don't stay away so long," she said, and Frank promised he wouldn't. As they pulled out of the barn lot, Della waved. For a moment, she thought T. Barry was awake and moving, but when she looked again, it was only Snapper in the back window trying to gnaw his way through the glass.

On Friday night, Della went to the Vacation Bible School Wiener Roast and Parents Program. She had not missed it in fifteen years. She arrived a few minutes before the program began, in time to see the artwork and crafts. In the chapel, she watched the children clap and nod their heads as they sang the familiar songs.

When the singing was over, the crowd moved outside, and Della joined them. She pulled a lawn chair next to the fire in the only open spot, one beside Mary Sue. For a long time, they roasted wieners without talking. When Mary Sue's stick began to burn, Della pointed it out, saving the littlest Peevy child's supper from the flames. "So," Mary Sue finally said. "How was your visit?" She looked tired. Bible School took its toll on the teachers.

"Good," said Della. "Same as always." She gave her roasted wiener to a passing child, then took a couple of marshmallows from the package and fastened them on her stick. "How about you? How'd it go this week?"

Mary Sue put her hand to her temple and shut her eyes. "Considering the fact that we were two teachers short and one of the craft shipments didn't come in, I'd say we did all right."

Della nodded.

Mary Sue gazed at the kids playing in the churchyard. "I don't know," she said. "Sometimes I think we're just wasting our time. Sometimes I wonder whether any of these kids take anything home at the end of the week besides their crafts."

Della watched a group of boys laugh and chase each other with hot marshmallows. The sun sank behind the trees, making it look as if the woods were on fire. "They're kids," said Della. "Maybe that's enough."

The
June
Woman

Dutchi Halliday sat at the Ophelia table in the hotel dining room, pretending to eat something elegant and expensive from the sugar bowl in front of her. "If you had it to do over again," Dutchi said to her mother, "I bet you would. Go somewhere important, I mean." Mrs. Halliday was not listening. She buzzed from table to table, lighting long enough to inspect the silverware. She acted like she had not heard a word that had been spoken to her.

"I bet that's what you'd do," Dutchi said, dipping her finger into the sugar again. Things tasted better at the Ophelia table, she decided. The sugar was always fresh, while the stuff on the other tables was as crusty as old snow. The Ophelia table, a mahogany piece that seated six, used to belong to Miss Ophelia Simmons. It came out of her house when she died, and now it belonged to Mrs. Halliday. It was the only table in the hotel covered with a lace cloth instead of cigarette burns. It was also the only table without chicken grease and chewing gum wads on the underside. Mrs. Halliday was proud of her table and reserved it for tourists who occasionally passed through Farlanburg on their way to other places. Dutchi, although not yet a tourist herself, was fond of sitting there.

"Would you?" Dutchi asked. "Want to go places if you still had the chance? I bet you probably would. What do you think? Huh?" Dutchi imagined she was a tourist from some big city. She arched her brows and pulled in her cheeks until her jaws ached. She felt very New Yorky today.

Mrs. Halliday stopped. She sucked hard on her cigarette, flipped the ashes into a vase of plastic flowers, then squinted at her daughter through the smoke. Sugar crystals lay like dandruff on the girl's shoulders and chest. Her small hands dropped white flecks down the front of her jacket. The garment, a black, well-tailored thing, had been left behind by a guest at the hotel. On its original owner, it had looked sensual, with a neckline that plunged to reveal an abundance of cream-colored flesh. On Dutchi's small body, the neckline still plunged, but it revealed mostly freckles.

"You get a kick outa this, don't you?" Mrs. Halliday finally said.

Dutchi stared at her mother.

"Why is it you always try to make it sound like I'm some kind of nothing? Like I never been anywhere? I been places, you know," said Mrs. Halliday as she strode toward a corner table. She was a tall woman who walked with her pelvis thrust forward and her shoulders thrown back as though a cross-wind blew each half of her body in a different direction. She often joked that her posture had been her downfall because the top half of her always got there too late to protest what the bottom half had already done.

"Before you were born, your daddy and me went lots of places. To Cleveland to see Aunt Woots. To Baltimore when your daddy worked in the shipyards. Lots of places. And what about that trip to Reno with Norm? Or doesn't that count in your book?"

It counted all right, Dutchi thought. To Reno with Mr. Jarrett. To Pittsburgh with Walt. To some stupid car race in Tennessee with Harold someone before him. Those trips counted all right, Dutchi thought, as she continued to stare at her mother and the cigarette that dangled between Mrs. Halliday's lips like it was ingrown and now a part of her face. Lately, it bothered Dutchi when her mother smoked. It wasn't so much the smoking as the way she did it. Why did she have to suck in her jaws when she took a puff and make it look like she was trying to get something impossible from the cigarette? Why did she have to do lots of things that she did, like dyeing her hair the color of a fox squirrel? Mrs. Halliday's hair, like the rest of her, lived for men, Dutchi knew. For the time being, that man was Norm Jarrett. If he had wanted Mrs. Halliday to look like a skunk, Mrs. Halliday would willingly have obliged him.

Dutchi sighed. "I wasn't talking about shipyards. You just don't understand the kind of places I'm talking about."

"I understand enough to know that the sooner you get what you got *in* your head *out* of your head, the better off you're gonna be," Mrs. Halliday said, frowning at her daughter. "You ain't the first person to ever bust a gut trying to find your way in this world, Dutchi. You think I can't tell you a thing or two about the way you're feeling? You think I can't tell you what it's like to be young and aching because you want the whole pie? I been young, you know, and let me tell you something: You'll settle! One of these days, you'll look around you and realize you can't have it all, and when that day comes, you'll learn to be happy with just a slice. And if you can't have a slice, you'll settle for the crumbs!" Having done her duty, Mrs. Halliday squared her shoulders and looked rather pleased with herself.

"I don't want crumbs!" Dutchi said, fighting tears. "I just want to go somewhere. You know. Where things can happen to me. We could, you know! We could take out of here right now and never come back. We could go someplace you've always wanted to go."

Mrs. Halliday laughed. "I don't want to go anywhere else. Things are happening for me right here in Farlanburg, baby. Good things for a change." She winked at Dutchi. "Why would I want to mess it all up by going somewhere else just because my baby has growing pains? You'll get over it," she said. "I promise." Mrs. Halliday began to peer and pick at something between the tines of a fork. She was still scratching at the fork, her head surrounded by a halo of blue smoke, when Dutchi left the room.

Dutchi went out on the front porch, sat down on the steps, and put her head on her knees. "I hope I never get over *any*thing!" she said, and she whispered the words several times to make sure that whatever it was that made people get over things didn't creep up on her and take her by surprise. She thought about the wink her mother had given her. She hated it when someone winked at her like that. It was one of those "we've been through a lot together, kid" kind of winks that grown-ups like to give you as a sign they think you're old enough to share their underwear. It made her feel like she was in cahoots about things she didn't even think were worth cahooting about.

It was true—she and her mother had been through a lot together. "Men troubles," Mrs. Halliday had always called it.

But for Dutchi, the words had always translated to mean *her* standing in some dark hallway listening to Jack or Walt or whoever telling her mother to hit the road, then *her* putting her hands over her ears to keep from hearing her mother beg for another chance, just one more chance to prove what a woman she could be.

"We're having men troubles," Dutchi used to repeat at school, before she got some sense and learned to keep quiet. It was her way of explaining why she was moving again. The words, when she said them, always sounded so clean and far-removed from the dirty scene that had caused her to say them in the first place. No, nothing good could come from a wink that made you remember things you just wanted to forget, Dutchi knew.

"Slices and crumbs!" she snorted now, wondering why there were so many things lately she wanted to forget. "Pressed," she had been calling her new condition, and when she felt that way, which was often, she would lie on her back on her bed, walk her bare feet up the walls, and pretend she was going places. Faraway places. Like China. Or Chicago. Sometimes she wished her stubby toes would reach the ceiling so she could hang like a bat and let her depression drain from a hole in the top of her head. It would be thick, brown, and horrid-smelling, she knew—a sure sign that some part of her was wasting within.

On particularly bad days, when it was rainy and there was nothing else to do, she went down to Brown & Canadine's and tried on brassieres. Big ones, like 36's.

"We have an excellent line for girls your age," Mrs. Canadine frequently reminded her, eyeing Dutchi's chest. Once she had offered Dutchi a stretchy little thing with pink chickens embroidered on the front.

"You're mistaken," Dutchi had replied, using all her savings for a 38D with cups as pointy as ice-cream cones.

Everybody was mistaken about her these days. Including Benny. Used to be they were friends and she thought he understood her, even though he was a year younger and she would not have expected him to. Used to be they could get mad and punch and kick and snot around but always know what they were punching about. Not anymore. Now she punched him because she needed to punch someone, and he was available. Some days, she punched him for things he could do nothing about—like the dimples in his knees or the baby fat that hung on him and made him look like he had breasts. Afterward, she'd punch him again for his hurt, bewildered look, which plainly showed he didn't understand. Some days, she wished she'd never been friends with him in the first place. Not that she'd had much choice. When her mother and Mr. Jarrett, Benny's father, had formed "the partnership" and moved to Farlanburg to manage the hotel together, she and Benny had been part of the merger. Since then, they had eaten their meals together at the same Formica table, spent the long summer days together throwing rocks at each other at the gravel pit, and learned to smile and nod together whenever anyone referred to Mrs. Halliday as Mrs. Jarrett. All that togetherness had been enough to make them friends. Sort of. They were still sort of friends, Dutchi knew, but something was changing. Benny said it was her. She hoped he was right.

Hot weather made Mrs. Halliday huffy. It ruined her customers' appetites, she said. Hot Thursdays were particularly bad because Thursdays were just naturally slow anyway since most folks were saving themselves to let loose on Friday. That's what Mrs. Halliday always told people who came into the hotel to eat on Thursday and found themselves eating alone. It was her way of letting them know there was nothing wrong with the food—that her cooking was just as clean on one day as another.

This Thursday was no exception. By late afternoon, the dining room was still deserted, except for Mrs. Halliday, who leaned like a limp dandelion across the reception desk and waited without looking like she knew what she was waiting for. Outside, the maples showed their silver-bellied leaves to the sky and writhed in a wind as hot as if an oven had been opened and left on.

Dutchi sat cross-legged on the front porch, playing a game of crazy eights with Benny, who lay sprawled and flush-faced beside her. "You can't play hearts on top of spades," Benny was saying. "Anytime I put down spades, Dutchi, you got to play spades. That's the rules. You can't just go dumping any old thing you want on top of my spades."

Dutchi was not listening. Her attention was focused on a cream-colored car that had pulled up in front of the hotel. "Ssshhh," she said, fanning herself with her cards and keeping her eyes on the car. Benny turned to look, and together they watched a woman in a dark blue suit get out of the car, arch her back like a cat, then shut the door behind her. She took off her sunglasses and looked around as if she were seeing something she'd never seen before. Spotting Dutchi and Benny on the porch, she hesitated, then walked toward them, her shoes making a rich click, click, clicking sound on the sidewalk. At the edge of the porch, she stopped and placed two of the whitest hands Dutchi had even seen on the banister. "Who's winning?" she asked.

Dutchi and Benny looked at the woman and then at each other. "Me," Benny finally said, smiling until his eyes became

slits. "I'm gonna beat the socks off her—if she'll stop dumping hearts on top of my spades and play like she's supposed
to."

The woman shifted her eyes to Dutchi and stared until
Dutchi looked at the floor. She was the kind of woman you
didn't dare look at too long, Dutchi knew, because if you did,
you'd be there looking all day. Her eyes, which were large and
gray, were lined with black and would have looked like a
raccoon's if they hadn't been so pretty. Her lips were the
color of the pokeberries that used to grow behind Ophelia
Simmons' garage. They were good lips, Dutchi thought, and
not the poochy kind that spread all over the faces of some of
the women she knew. The woman kept her lips pulled in tight
like she knew a secret but wasn't going to tell. She reminded
Dutchi of the women in the catalogs that Dutchi kept under
her bed—tall, willowy women who looked hungry but happy
being that way.

"Could you tell me how I might get back to Highway 112?"
she asked. Her voice sounded like her throat was lined with
fur. She didn't slop the numbers together either and say "one-
twelve" the way most of the people Dutchi knew said it.
Instead, she took her time, pursed her lips, and pronounced
each number as though it were the most important thing in
the world. "One hundred and twelve" was the way she said it,
and Dutchi knew that everybody ought to say it that way. She
suddenly hated every word that had ever come out of her
mouth and vowed never to speak again.

Benny was looking at the woman and shaking his head.

"I want to go to Prattsville," the woman said.

"Oh!" said Benny, and as he gave directions and pointed
his stubby fingers and acted like he had been to Prattsville
every day of his life, Dutchi was ashamed of him and couldn't

understand why he couldn't see he was just making a fool of himself. She saw the dirt under his fingernails and hoped the woman wouldn't notice. She didn't look like the type of woman who would appreciate having dirty fingernails waved in front of her face.

Dutchi could stand it no longer. "This is the road that will take you to Highway—to Prattsville," she said, shoving Benny's hand aside. She didn't recognize the sound of her own voice. "You ought to be there by midnight, I'm certain, if your car doesn't give you difficulties."

Benny wrinkled his nose and turned his head toward Dutchi as though he had a stiff neck. She glared back at him, and it was a glare that carried the promise of a punch if he opened his mouth.

The woman watched them both. "I had no idea it would be that far," she said, frowning. She shaded her eyes with her hands and turned her face toward the sun, which looked like a dirty orange beach ball stuck in the top of a willow tree.

"It is," Dutchi said. "It's every bit that far. Miles, I guess. You have several mountains to cross, and besides that, you have to go past a prison."

At this, Benny's mouth fell open, and his upper lip no longer covered his teeth. But the woman didn't seem to notice, because she was laughing. Dutchi laughed, too, although she didn't know why.

"If I had known that, I certainly would never have come this way," the woman said. "It serves me right for traveling without a map."

"You do need a map," Dutchi agreed. "I never travel without one."

"Well," said the woman, "I suppose I'll have to stay here then."

Dutchi shrugged and looked away. Suit yourself, she wanted her look to say.

"Is there anyone inside?" the woman asked.

Dutchi scrambled to her feet, opened the door, and smiled. Inside, it was all she could do to leave the woman at the reception desk. When two people had as much to say to each other as they did, they needed a lifetime to say it. But the woman was tired, Dutchi could tell, and there would be plenty of time for talk later.

"It's your turn," Dutchi said, after she had returned to the porch. But Benny only stared at her and chewed the skin on his upper lip.

"What kinda car do you think that is?" Dutchi asked.

"Some kind of a big one," said Benny. "Why'd you tell her that stuff about Prattsville? How do you know how far it is?"

"I just do, that's all," Dutchi said. "Go on and play."

Afterward, it wasn't so much the fear of getting caught that bothered Dutchi as the fact that she'd lied to a woman with a name like June Johnson. That's what the woman signed when she checked into the hotel, but she looked like she should've had a name like Carmalotta, Dutchi thought. Lying to a woman with a name like Carmalotta would have been a whole lot easier on the conscience than lying to a woman with a name as straightforward as June Johnson.

"Falsifying," Mr. Jarrett would have called it. He would have grinned and shown his big, yellow teeth when he said it and looked real pleased with himself like he thought he was a big-time lawyer or something.

Mrs. Halliday would not have worried about such a little lie in the least, Dutchi felt sure, but then Mrs. Halliday was not a worrier. "It's all in how you look at things," she would have said as she frequently did after telling a carload of prospective guests that there wasn't another hotel within miles. What she said wasn't true, but that was not the point. "Responsibility is what we're talking here," she always said. "It just doesn't make sense to send folks away when they're tired and might run off the road and say to themselves just before they died that those people back in Farlanburg were a pack of irresponsible liars." Dutchi knew *she* didn't want to be responsible for anything bad happening to anyone, especially to a woman like June Johnson. It was, she supposed, all in how you looked at things.

Dutchi's mother had other sayings, too, and one of Mrs. Halliday's favorites was "There's more to owning a name than just having a face to stick behind it." Mrs. Halliday fretted a lot because she didn't get to use her "clever" sayings much in Farlanburg. They just didn't seem to apply to anyone she knew. But she recognized an opportunity when one checked into her hotel. That's exactly what she told Dutchi and Benny later that evening after June Johnson had come down from her room and gone for a walk up the street. Mrs. Halliday said she could recognize a liar when she saw one and that she'd bet her bottom dollar June Johnson wasn't really June Johnson at all but someone who just picked that name like she was drawing names for Christmas out of a dirty hat.

"That woman ain't a bit more of a June Johnson than I am," she snorted, as she stood in the kitchen stirring a pot of beans and holding the curtain back so she could watch the woman walk up the street. "Look at her. She even walks like she ain't real. Like one of those store dummies." Tossing her head, Mrs. Halliday abandoned her beans and went tripping across the kitchen like a swaybacked fairy.

"I don't think she looks like a June woman, either," said

Benny, sulking and stirring his plate of beans.

"I bet she's just who she says she is, and if she isn't, it's because her real name is too important to tell," Dutchi said. She watched the woman from a window at the rear of the kitchen, then closed her eyes and imagined herself beside her. She could hear the click, click, clicking of their heels on the sidewalk and feel the coolness of silk things against their skin.

"You'd have thought she'd at least have let me know whether she'd be taking her meal in the dining room," Mrs. Halliday grumbled.

"People like her don't eat after four o'clock. They only have a drink and maybe something light," Dutchi said, having no idea what something light might be.

Mrs. Halliday made a snarling noise. "If the woman can't recognize good food when she smells it cooking, then she wouldn't recognize her own name if it jumped out and bit her. She can call herself June Johnson all she wants. I know better!" With that, Mrs. Halliday picked up four plates of beans, loaded them onto her arms until she looked like an octopus, then disappeared into the dining room, letting the doors swing shut behind her.

"It's okay if she's a liar," Benny said. "At least *she's* a pretty liar. Liar, liar, pants on fire," he chanted, pointing a finger at Dutchi.

Mr. Jarrett, who suddenly appeared in the doorway that led to the back porch, made kissing noises as he rolled his eyes and danced toward the stove. Ooh la la, he wanted to meet this June Johnson gal, he said. "Especially if she's a good-looker," he added, winking wildly at Benny.

The sun had long since slipped behind the black rim of the hills when Dutchi bounded down the steps at the back of the hotel with a sweater in her hand and two quarters in each of her shoes. Dark clouds hurried across the sky, and the leaves fanned the air like thousands of black, waving hands. Dutchi smiled. She would be leaving this place soon, she knew, and going off to live the kind of life she was meant to live. Everyone who knew her would be more than a little sorry to see her going. "We always knew there was something different about that girl," the people in town would say, and former teachers would recall minor incidents that showed early signs of her going.

Dutchi shivered with excitement. It was scary to be alone on the street this time of night without so much as your shadow for company. All the stores closed at six o'clock, unless you counted the grocery store, but she felt sure there was no need to check in there. A woman like June Johnson wouldn't waste her time staring at a bunch of tin cans and heads of cabbage.

It had to be the Alibi Inn or the River Lounge, she decided, but she felt sure it wasn't the Inn, because it served mostly cheeseburgers and beer. The thought of a woman like June Johnson having to eat cheeseburgers and getting grease all over her lips and chin was enough to make Dutchi sick.

The River Lounge was a new place at the end of town owned by Wendell Stalnaker, one of Mr. Jarrett's buddies. Dutchi had been in there once or twice when her mother had sent her to find Mr. Jarrett. It was a flashy place at night, with blue lights on the roof and a portable sign that blinked on and off by the side of the road: "Excitement . . . Fine Dining . . . Entertainment . . . The River Lounge!" In the daytime, the sign didn't flash at all, unless you looked back at it as you were heading out of town. Then it said, "Rent this sign!" That was before someone knocked the "g" out.

Inside the lounge, there was a jukebox that wailed real

heart-hurting songs about women who married no-account men and spent the rest of their lives going to Fist City just to keep them. The tables were decorated with candles stuck in bottles, giving the place a wicked jack-o'-lantern look when you peeped in.

That's where Dutchi found her—in a booth in the back section of the River Lounge. She was there, but she didn't look like she belonged there, and Dutchi felt strangely relieved. She sat alone, staring out the window, looking very foreign and forbidden. She reminded Dutchi of a statue she had seen once in a jewelry store: a white, fragile-looking thing kept behind glass so you could not touch it or see how much it cost. Seeing her like that, Dutchi didn't think she looked like the kind of woman who would understand a lie.

The sight of the woman and the smell of booze-filled bodies were enough to make Dutchi's head spin as she stepped inside. Wendell Stalnaker was standing behind the bar laughing and talking to two men. He didn't seem to notice that an unusual woman was sitting alone in the back section of his lounge, staring out his window. A woman who looked like June Johnson could've sat anywhere in Wendell Stalnaker's lounge and done anything she pleased, Dutchi supposed. She didn't need a man's permission.

"Hi ya, Dutch," Wendell yelled when he saw Dutchi at the door. Dutchi threw up her hand. She didn't like Wendell Stalnaker very much. She didn't like any of Mr. Jarrett's buddies very much. "Your old man ain't been in tonight," Wendell said.

Dutchi shook her head. He ain't my old man, she wanted to say. "I have to talk to *her,*" she said instead, smiling and pointing toward the June woman. She was relieved when Wendell shrugged and returned to his conversation at the bar.

She emptied the money from her shoes and bought two root beers from the machine by the door. Then she made her way toward the back.

As she walked, her eyes were drawn to the crease visible where the woman's jacket made a **V** and to the gold-colored buttons, which shone like lights advertising an attraction. Streams of smoke as clean and straight as arrows came from her lips, and Dutchi knew she was looking at a woman who had been born to sit in lounges all over the world and to smoke cigarettes the way they were meant to be smoked. Here was a woman who didn't smoke stubs or spew smoke and make it look as though a brushfire were being fought inside her head. She made it look so pretty!

With her pop bottles in her hands, Dutchi slid into a booth across the room from the woman and waited. She took a deep breath and began to count. It was a good idea to count before you struck up a conversation with strangers, she had learned. Otherwise, they might think you were too eager or didn't have any friends, and they'd just up and leave. Normally, taking it to five was good enough, but this time was special, so Dutchi held out for ten. As she counted, she tried hard to remember the chapter on introductions from her English book. She didn't really need an introduction, she knew. How many times had she pulled such a woman from under her bed and studied her far into the night, until she could almost read the thoughts behind the expression frozen forever on the woman's face? June Johnson didn't know that, but she would soon, along with a thousand other things Dutchi had waited a lifetime to tell somebody.

She could almost see the pictures of the two men in suits in her textbook now. They were smiling and shaking hands, and there was a third person, a blonde woman, to help them. "Mr.

Smith, meet Mr. Jones. Mr. Jones, this is Mr. Smith," the red letters below the picture said. They all looked as if they knew what they were doing. There was a right way and a wrong way to do these things, Dutchi knew, and with a woman like June Johnson, you wanted to do it right.

Dutchi closed her eyes and took a deep breath as she finished her counting. The whole room seemed to spin as she got out of her seat. She reminded herself to speak slowly. If the words came out too fast, it might sound as if she'd said them so many times to so many people that they no longer meant anything.

"Hello, June Johnson. This is Dutchi Halliday," she whispered to herself for practice. As soon as the words were out of her mouth, she knew they didn't sound right, but there was no time to figure out why. Her legs had carried her faster than she'd planned, and she was now so close to the woman's table that if she stumbled, she would fall on her. The woman was looking at her and smiling in a strange way, and Dutchi knew that there would be no need for an introduction after all. She held up the pop bottles and smiled back, and it was the kind of smile that felt as if might split her face from ear to ear. But she didn't care. The two of them were together smiling at each other and nothing else mattered until Dutchi realized that three of them were smiling, the third being Fud Larson, who smiled from the bar. The longer Dutchi stood there, the less a part of the smiling she began to feel, but the same legs that had brought her to the woman's table seemed reluctant to take her away again.

It was Fud Larson who finally broke the spell. Dutchi watched him pick up two drinks from the bar, and with the ease of a man who's done such a thing every day of his life, he walked over and sat down in the same booth as the June woman. Dutchi waited for the woman to move. She did not. Instead, she looked directly at Dutchi and gave her an under- wear-sharing wink that Dutchi knew she'd remember far lon- ger than anything she'd ever read in her textbooks.

Fud Larson with the wavy hair! Fud Larson with his thick legs turned out at the calves like he'd been riding horses all day! Fud Larson with the clodhopper boots and curly lips on a mouth so foul it could put even Mr. Jarrett to shame! Dutchi could do nothing but stare at them as they sat there acting like there was nothing or nobody in the whole world that mattered except themselves. She watched them as they narrowed their eyes and looked each other over like excited cats—watched them as they smiled those twosome kind of smiles that clearly told her there was no room for a threesome.

Suddenly, she felt sick, sick in a way she hadn't been since she was five and vomited behind her mask at Halloween. As she walked toward the door, she was conscious of nothing but the cigarette smoke, liquor fumes, and scattered chairs that seemed determined to keep her in the lounge as long as possi- ble. The next minute, the River Lounge was nothing more than a blue eye winking in the distance behind her.

Later, as Dutchi lay on her back on her bed, she listened to the hiss of crickets in the night air and waited for the sound she knew would come. When it did, it did not bring with it the feeling of loss she had expected—but all the comfort of a song with a familiar tune.

She heard the bump, bump, bumping of his boots on the stairway and, finally, the hollow, uneven clicking of the woman's shoes. And when she had finished hearing all she could stand to hear, she closed her eyes, put her feet on the wall, and tried to think about going places. Faraway places.

Instead, she thought of the people she had known and the places they had seen. Mostly, she thought of Harold, who was before Walt, who was before Mr. Jarrett. Harold, who never went anywhere except to car races. Never anywhere important like to New York to see the statue or to an ocean to watch the waves wash the beaches clean. It was not that those things were so far away, Harold used to say. Other things were simply closer. And she now knew with the certainty of a well-seasoned traveler that Harold, for once, had been right.

Rabbit
in the
Foot

When Evelyn called her sister Jean to tell her about the overnight trip to Charleston, she had to settle for Tootles, one of Jean's renters. Jean couldn't come to the phone.

"She's in the bathtub," said Tootles in a voice so scratchy she might have eaten a Brillo pad. "I'm here. Wanna tell me?"

For a moment, Evelyn considered hanging up. She would have if she hadn't lost her husband Leo six months ago, making Jean her only relative within miles. At sixty, Evelyn wanted to be close to her sister, share memories with someone who had known her way back when. Jean's husband had run out on her years ago. Two sisters: they needed each other. Evelyn wasn't about to let some renter stand in their way.

"If you must know," said Evelyn, "I'm planning a trip."

"Oooh," said Tootles. "How exciting! Where you going?"

"Not *me*. *We*. Jean and I." Evelyn sighed. She wasn't sure how much she wanted Tootles to know. Tootles had rented from Jean for years. She drank too much and had hair the color of Orange Crush. Rumor was she dated married men.

"She's all right," Jean always said whenever the subject came up. "She's just been knocked around a bit." Jean said that about all her renter friends. They shared her kitchen, her washcloths, her life.

"You don't know anything about them," Evelyn argued. "One morning you'll wake up with a *disease* or with your throat slit from ear to ear."

"There are worse things," said Jean.

"I'd like to know what!" Evelyn huffed. Leo was alive at the time, and all two hundred ten pounds of his presence had stood between Evelyn and an understanding of what Jean had meant.

"Leave my renters to me," Jean said. "They're harmless. There's not a one of them wouldn't give you the shirt off his back."

The way those shirts usually smelled, Evelyn wasn't sure she'd want one.

Normally, she would have left a message or told Tootles to have Jean call her back, but she hadn't talked to a soul in almost three days. She was afraid she'd start bugging the operator every hour pretending to want the time or loll at her kitchen table and dial 4444 to hear someone read the weather. Evelyn lived in Farlanburg; Jean, in Clendenin. Clendenin was just across the county line, but it was still long distance. It irked Evelyn that she had to pay money to talk to her sister when she was practically within shouting range.

She propped the receiver between her head and shoulder

and picked up an emery board. She hadn't planned to divulge any of the particulars about the trip, but once she got started, she couldn't stop.

"There wasn't a word in the paper," Evelyn found herself saying. "I'd never have known a thing about it if I hadn't overheard a conversation at the IGA."

The trip was sponsored by the Farlanburg Senior Citizens' Center. Evelyn did *not* consider herself a senior citizen, and she hoped no one would pronounce her guilty by association. Besides, the Center opened their tours to anyone when they couldn't round up enough members to book a trip.

"Sounds like a bladder bus to me," said Tootles.

"What?" Evelyn mashed her ear against the receiver to try to hear through the crackling on the line. She had a bad connection.

"Bladder bus," said Tootles. "You know. Old people stopping every five minutes to pee. You could crawl to Charleston and back before you'd get there with that crew."

Evelyn paused, emery board in hand. She tried to think of a clever comeback, but she was so flustered that nothing came to mind. She decided just to sit there till Jean came to the phone, and she didn't care if it took all day and half the night. Twenty-six cents for the first minute, eighteen for each additional minute. She'd checked it out before.

Tootles laughed. "You still there?"

"Go away," said Evelyn. "I'm waiting for Jean."

Four minutes. Five minutes. Six. Leo would've had a fit.

A horrible scene began to form in Evelyn's mind. She could see Jean floating face down in the bathtub. Jean's curls moved like old grass in deep water; her body bobbed like a cork. Jean. Her baby sister. Drowned by the hairy hands of a renter and Evelyn powerless to stop it.

Evelyn shut her eyes and tried to concentrate on the sounds she could hear through the receiver: TV, music, traffic. She thought she heard splashing in the background, the frantic thump of knees and elbows making waves on a porcelain shore. Finally, she heard laughter, then Jean's voice as she picked up the phone.

"Evelyn?"

"Jean? Is that you?" Evelyn's hand flew to her chest. "Thank heavens you're all right! I was so worried about you all alone in that house!"

"I ain't alone," said Jean. "Tootles is here and Spider Legs and Cuttler."

"Sshhh!" said Evelyn. She began to file fingernails like she was felling trees with a handsaw. "Don't say their names or let on like we're talking about them. Just act natural."

"What?" said Jean.

"You take people in. You don't know a thing about them. Spider Legs. Cuttler. Normal people don't have names like that. You don't even know what those names might mean!"

"Hell I don't," said Jean. "I gave them those names myself."

Evelyn stopped sawing and frowned.

"Surely you didn't call to talk about that," said Jean.

Evelyn paused, trying to determine how badly she'd hurt her chances of getting Jean to accompany her on the trip. She laid out the details and played up the mall excursion and capitol tour. "There's a chance we might get to tour the governor's mansion," she said. "See the governor. Wouldn't that be nice?"

Jean was silent. For a moment, Evelyn thought she'd been cut off. "Well?"

"Sounds great," said Jean. "You've talked about doing

something like this for years. You oughta go."

Evelyn gave her thumbnail a couple of quick passes. "How long's it been since we took a trip together? Forty, fifty years? It'll give us a chance to talk. Like sisters ought to."

"Nah," said Jean. "You better count me out."

"Come on. You're dying to go. I can hear it in your voice."

"Right now isn't such a good time for me," said Jean.

"It's money, isn't it? Let me loan it to you. It's cheaper when there's two. They give the second person this big discount, and you share a room."

"Why don't you ask someone from your church?"

"They're going. With their husbands. Everyone's got a partner except me." Evelyn fiddled with the phone cord. "Please?" she said weakly.

"Oh," said Jean. "I . . . oh."

"This has been a rough year for me," Evelyn said.

Jean moaned. "Oh, all right," she said at last.

"You won't regret it," Evelyn told her. "I'll make sure of that. We'll get ourselves some new clothes. Doll up. We'll be the two best-looking women on the bus."

"Who'll be there to notice?" said Jean.

When Evelyn got off the phone, she went into the kitchen and downed half a can of Beanie Weenies. She couldn't decide whether she was depressed or in the mood to celebrate. She pulled a loose bobby pin from her hair, opened it with her teeth, and caught a glimpse of herself in the toaster. With her hair in pincurls, she looked like someone had played a game of X's and O's on her head. She kept her hair in pincurls a lot since Leo died. She wanted to be ready in case she decided to go out and eat or she found out about a sale in progress at the mall.

Leo had been the stay-at-home sort. A trip to Western Steer one Saturday night a month, and he was satisfied. Leo was a veteran. An army man. He'd traipsed all over Europe during the war before he married Evelyn, and when he came home in '45, he swore he'd never leave the state again. With the exception of a trip to Nashville he had to make if he wanted to keep his job at the farm equipment dealership, Leo had been a man of his word.

He used to get in a bad mood every time Evelyn got the urge to go somewhere. She'd read in the paper about trips her friends had taken, slide presentations they were giving in the basement at church. Just reading about their adventures was enough to cause Evelyn's cheeks to flush, her heart to palpitate. She and Leo had had a good marriage, as far as marriages go, but nothing he'd ever done to her, even in their most intimate moments, had achieved quite the same effect.

"There's something wrong with your heart," he used to tell her, his big red ear pressed against her chest.

"Well then, Dr. Kildare, you just tell me why it only happens when I'm thinking about going somewhere," Evelyn snapped.

Once, in an attempt to improve Evelyn's lovemaking, Leo had even asked her to pretend they were doing what they were doing on a plane bound for "... Jerusalem!" he had cried in frustration. But that hadn't worked because, married or not, Evelyn felt guilty doing what she was doing if she was anywhere near the Holy Land.

Evelyn stood up to Leo once, told him she didn't think it was fair he got his traveling out of his system before he married her.

"My memory's good," he said, rubbing his big head. "Name a place. I'll tell you anything you want to know."

"Don't you want me to see some of the places you fought during the war? Go with you to some of your old stomping grounds?" Evelyn pleaded.

Leo smiled that big lopsided smile of his and said he'd shoot her legs off if she ever brought it up again. Leo liked to play the old soldier role and joke around like that. Just the same, Evelyn never brought it up again. Sometimes she tried to remember how his face had looked when he said it. Lately, she thought her memory was going because the face she remembered looked downright mean.

Evelyn jumped as her cat, Orville, arched his back and rubbed against her legs. "Here, lazy thing. Stuff yourself," she said, dumping the rest of the Beanie Weenies onto his plate. She rubbed his thick, yellow back and looked at the hairs on her hands. Leo had hated cats. He never let her have one. Orville's timing had been just right. He stalked onto her porch one week to the day after Leo died. When Evelyn opened the screen door to see what the cat would do, it ran into the house, hopped into Leo's chair, curled up, and went to sleep. Beat anything Evelyn had ever seen. She was a Baptist, had attended the Baptist church downtown for years, and she was not one to condone talk of reincarnation. But she had her suspicions about that cat. At the time, Orville Redenbacher was advertising popcorn on TV. Evelyn gave the cat the first name she could think of. She was afraid if she waited too long, the cat would smile and say, "Call me Leo."

She stared out the dining room window while Orville picked the weenies out of the beans. Strange how he took what he wanted and left the rest. Almost human. She was going to do the same, she decided, with the rest of her life. Have the weenies for a change. Let someone else eat the beans.

She tapped her fingers on the table and tried to figure out what she could do to make the day pass faster. Widow, be strong, she told herself. That's what Brother Bennett, the pastor at her church, had said. Brother Bennett had her on his prayer list. Half the church had her on their prayer lists. Evelyn would have settled for a phone call or a visit.

She pulled back her curtain and surveyed her yard. Spring was on its way. Her forsythia was just about to bloom, and there was an intensity to the afternoon sunlight that made the world seem new. It was a world where anything could happen. She'd take this trip, and as soon as the weather got warmer, she'd get out of the house and go somewhere every day. She'd spend more time with Jean.

Jean had changed lately. Gotten nicer. Maybe it had something to do with age. They talked on the phone three or four times a week. Evelyn did the calling, but that didn't bother her a bit. She had never been one to quibble over turns.

"You just called me on Monday," Jean sometimes said if Evelyn called again on Wednesday afternoon.

"Did I?" Evelyn said, cheerfully. "I don't mind."

And she didn't. She didn't mind anything about Jean these days except the renters. Jean usually kept four or five. Her house was huge and slightly run-down, with rusted drain spouts and rotten boards on the front and back porches. There were enough rooms for all the losers in Clendenin to have a place to stay. They came and went, changing with the seasons. During the years, Evelyn had come to think of Jean's house as Noah's ark. At least two of everything had lived there.

Evelyn had a plan. She hadn't told Jean about it yet. She was saving that for the trip. She wanted them to get a place together, something small, inexpensive. Maybe rent an apartment in town. An apartment big enough for just two sisters would be the berries. There would be no room for three.

Tootles had run Jean's life long enough. Tootles poured cream in Evelyn's coffee when Evelyn came to visit; she knew where the matches were kept and which drawers contained which spoons. She was pushy was what she was.

"Tootles!" Leo used to say. "What the hell kind of a name is that?" Leo had a lot to say about Jean and the way she lived her life. "She's got a big mouth," he said. "No man wants to live with a bossy woman." Leo used to say that Jean was jealous because Evelyn had always had better luck: with her marriage, her kids, the whole bit. Unlike Jean's ex, Leo was a good provider. He prided himself on that. "The wife and kids have never wanted for a thing," he liked to brag when he got a beer in him.

Jean had never liked Leo either. "He ain't my type," she once said.

"Oh, come on," Evelyn pressed. "Be specific."

"Specifically," said Jean, "I hate his guts."

"Jean hates all men." That's what Leo said. Leo had insight into women. It was a gift, he often said. He'd had it since birth.

He could have been right about Jean. Jean had made some bad choices. She'd had her share of trouble with men. She ran off at sixteen and married a man named Harry Noons, a black-haired, black-eyed fellow from Pennsylvania who talked a lot about cars. Jean stuck by him even though he beat her, "tuned her up" as he called it, once a week. He finally left her. Just drove off one afternoon in a red Mustang convertible he'd bought with money Jean had saved before she married. The state police found the car in Florida. Jean was afraid if they looked too hard, they might find Harry. They never did.

Evelyn felt sure the scandal would've killed her if she'd been in Jean's situation. But Jean was a tough one. She got a job as a dispatcher for a trucking company, started renting out rooms, and lived, instead. She had herself to think of—and Little Harry. Little Harry was only fourteen at the time. A sweet boy. He didn't stay sweet long. By the time he was fifteen, he'd bloodied the nose of every kid on the block. At seventeen, he robbed a Handi-Mart store. Used a pellet pistol. Said he didn't think that'd count.

Jean was afraid Little Harry would be sent away. She went to the store manager and asked what it would take to make it up. He knew a pretty woman when he saw one, so he showed her. He even threw in a job for Little Harry. But Little Harry got caught stealing candy. That was the only time, since they'd been grown, that Evelyn ever remembered hearing Jean cry.

"He loses his job over a lousy Three Musketeers bar!" Jean said, sobbing into the phone. "Do you know what he told them when they asked what he had to say for himself? He said, 'I like it.'"

"Stealing?" Evelyn asked, horrified.

"No!" said Jean, crying harder. "Candy!"

"We don't need this," said Leo, when Evelyn repeated the story to him. "I don't want you talking to her on the damn phone!"

"I just can't turn my back on her," Evelyn argued. "She's my sister."

"And I'm your husband!" yelled Leo, jabbing his thumb into his chest. "People get what they deserve, and we deserve a good life," he said, although he never said just what they'd done to deserve it. He put his arm around Evelyn's shoulders. "Jean is trouble, hon, and her kind of trouble is catching. I don't want her giving it to you."

Evelyn tried to protest, but with Leo, it didn't do much good.

"Think about it," he said.

Evelyn did. She had a husband. Good kids. Great kids. Better than Jean's kid. Maybe it was smart not to risk messing that up. Get mixed up in someone else's family problems, they'll end up blaming you.

When Jean called and Leo wasn't there, Evelyn claimed she was busy and couldn't talk. On weekends, Leo answered the phone, and if it was Jean, he lied and said, "She's out." Meanwhile, Evelyn stood there staring at Leo's face for a clue to what Jean might be saying.

"I feel so guilty," said Evelyn, covering her mouth with her hands.

"It's either me or her," said Leo. "You choose."

Evelyn sighed as she watched Orville lick the last bite of weenies from his plate. It was all so long ago. She and Leo had lived their kind of life. Jean had lived hers. The kids were grown. Daryl worked as an accountant in Denver, and Denny was married, had children, and was settled in Seattle. Neither of them had ever been in trouble with the law. They called her every three or four months and at Christmas.

Last time Jean had a letter from Little Harry, he wanted to borrow two hundred dollars. He'd divorced again and was working at a fruit stand in Texas. Little Harry said he sure missed home. Not a great kid, not even a good kid, but in a strange way, Evelyn sometimes thought it might be nice to have a son she could help, the way Jean helped Little Harry.

Evelyn sent in her fifty dollar deposit and called Jean to make sure she didn't forget. The entire trip was going to cost them each $99.95. Not bad, Evelyn thought, for everything it included. Leo would have croaked.

She brought his old brown suitcase down from the attic two weeks before the trip. She cut out a piece of paper, taped it to the suitcase, and wrote her name, address, and phone number on the slip. She'd heard those stories about travelers ending up in Chicago while their socks went on to Detroit. But the longer she thought about it, the more she worried. Finally, she ripped off the paper and threw it in the trash can. Anyone who could read well enough to *mail* her socks could *bring* them in person. No telling what kind of a creep might show up.

Soap, extra washcloths, deodorant, shampoo. All the little things had to be new. She arranged everything in the suitcase, stood back and inspected it, then rearranged it again and again. When she finally had it just right, she closed the lid, counted to ten, unsnapped the latches, and poked her head inside. How she loved the smell of a trip!

"Rabbit in the foot. That's what's wrong with you," Leo would've growled if he'd been there, and for one wicked moment, Evelyn was glad he was not. His rabbit saying was one he'd inherited from his father, who, like Leo, had never understood the need for travel. Leo's father used to say that travel was what was causing so many divorces. "It ain't good for people to see too much. Makes 'em dissatisfied with what they've got."

Evelyn had been to Baltimore once and to Akron to her Aunt Mamie's funeral in 1959. She did get to go to Nashville with Leo the time he went to the equipment convention, but that trip didn't really count because all she got to do was look at manure spreaders and big green tractors, and then she had to come straight home.

A sudden wave of shame washed over her. "Ungrateful woman," she knew Brother Bennett would have said if he could have read her mind. "Give thanks for the good life you've been given." That night, when Evelyn said her prayers, she asked God to forgive her for the ugly thoughts that sometimes popped into her head. She gave thanks for her children, for Jean, for the years she'd had with Leo, and said an extra thank-you for having been spared a marriage to a man like Harry Noons, who was a liar and a thief, a stinker who ran out on his wife and son. When Leo left her, he did it with class. Just slumped over at his desk one afternoon as he was closing a deal on one of those big green tractors. Turned out it was his heart they should have been listening to instead of hers.

Evelyn received her schedule a week before the trip. "Bus departs Farlanburg at 9:45 A.M. on Friday; arrives in Charleston, 12 noon." The part about arrivals and departures gave her goosebumps. Made her think of airports and jumbo jets.

That afternoon, she called Mrs. Garland Hornby to find out any last-minute details. Garland Hornby was a prominent realtor in town. Mrs. Hornby was the Senior Center Tour Coordination Chairwoman. That's what it always said below her picture, which was in the *Observer* almost every week. Mrs. Hornby was a well-traveled woman, and Evelyn felt awkward talking to her.

"Why so late?" Evelyn said when she got her on the phone.

"Beg your pardon?"

They were serving lunch at the center, Evelyn could tell. She could hear silverware clinking in the background. The Senior Center menu was published in the paper each week, and for some strange reason, Evelyn liked to read it. Today they were having meatloaf, boiled potatoes, mustard greens, and peach cobbler. Evelyn could almost taste it. She didn't cook much anymore, herself. Seemed silly to dirty so many dishes for just one.

"Why are we leaving so late?" Evelyn said. "If we got an earlier start, we'd get there sooner. Be able to pack more in."

Mrs. Hornby was nice about it. She blamed the late start on Allegheny Tours. "After all," she said, "they set this whole thing up. If you have any complaints, you'll have to take it up with them."

Evelyn had never liked to take anything up on the phone with people she didn't know. Leo had always taken care of that. She had no complaints, after all, she decided.

"We feel very fortunate to be able to offer this trip at such a low price," said Mrs. Hornby.

Evelyn agreed. She felt very fortunate to be able to take a trip at *any* price, but she didn't say it. She was not one to speak ill of the dead.

"It's a BLT," said Mrs. Hornby.

Evelyn was confused. She smelled bacon, envisioned tomatoes.

"BLTs are package deals. Darling little name, don't you think? It stands for Bargain Lovers' Tours. In case you didn't know." Mrs. Hornby cleared her throat. "Did you?" she said. "I bet you didn't know."

Evelyn tried to speak, but she seemed to have no voice. "I have to go," she said, hoarsely. "Someone's at my door," she lied, then hung up.

When Evelyn got off the phone, she had a headache and her stomach was in knots. She took an aspirin, then a Tums, and decided to stretch out on the living room couch and watch a little TV. Orville was asleep in the recliner. His yellow tail hung like a grapevine over the edge of the seat.

After all these months, Evelyn still couldn't bring herself to sit in the recliner. Leo had picked it out himself at the Bargain Barn. He must've sat in fifty or more before he found the right one. Evelyn still winced every time a sweeper salesman or Jehovah's Witness came in and sat down there.

She tried to relax, but her eyes wouldn't rest in their sockets. She spied the long, thin thread of a spider's web waving in a corner. March. And she hadn't even thought of spring cleaning. She had no plans to do any. Every year, since she'd been big enough to help her mama, she'd cleaned a house in the spring: repapered cupboards, painted bathrooms and kitchens, carried bedding out into the pale sunshine to air.

She'd given the house a good going over about a month after Leo died. Hired a girl from the domestic section of the classifieds to help her. They scrubbed the whole house with Lysol. Evelyn rubbed until her hands were raw, her eyes bloodshot from the fumes. Just before they finished, when they were on their hands and knees in the upstairs bathroom, the girl looked over at Evelyn. "I don't mean to be nosy," she said, "but did your husband have anything someone could catch?"

Evelyn began to laugh. She laughed all the way down the stairs, laughed until tears ran down her face, and only after she stepped outside and the November air hit her like a slap was she able to stop.

"You want me to help you box up his clothes?" the girl asked her. Evelyn decided against it. Six months later, she was still washing Leo's clean socks and ironing his unworn underwear.

Tuesday morning, three days before the trip, Evelyn called Jean. "You'll never guess what I forgot," she said.

Jean couldn't guess.

"Orville. What will I do with him while we're on the trip?"

"We'll only be gone a couple of days. Put out some extra food or have one of your neighbors come in and feed him."

"I don't like the idea of someone in my house."

"So, ask them to feed him on the porch."

"I can't do that. He's used to being fed inside."

Evelyn could hear Jean tapping on something.

"Leave the garage door open just a crack then."

Evelyn sighed. "I guess I could, but it's still so cold in there this time of year." She twisted the phone cord and stuck the loops on her fingers like rings. "Maybe this wasn't such a good idea," she said.

"It was *your* idea!" said Jean. "Do you want to go or not?"

"Course I do," said Evelyn. "What a silly thing to ask." She picked up a pen and began to doodle on the back of her phone book. "I want your opinion about something. I mean, I want you to tell me what you *really* think."

"About what?"

"This trip," said Evelyn. "Is it too soon? After Leo, I mean?"

"For God's sake!" said Jean. "The man's been dead for six months."

"Six months and fourteen days," said Evelyn. "You don't have to remind me." She drew several circles with her pen. "It's just . . . I don't want people saying I'm out kicking up my heels too soon after Leo . . . you know."

"The only one I know who would've said something like that was Leo, and he ain't apt to say much of anything anymore. You were a good wife to that—to him for more than forty years, Evelyn. Live a little while you've got the chance."

"Yeah," said Evelyn. "I suppose you're right. Do you think you're right?"

"You're right," said Jean. "That's almost word for word what she said."

Around six that evening, it started to rain. Evelyn closed the windows and latched the screen to the back porch, but left the door open so she could hear Orville when he scratched to get in. She sat at her kitchen table and watched the rain bounce off the surface of the road. There was usually a gully washer followed by a cold snap this time of year. She always thought of it as the Easter squall. It was a sign, Brother Bennett said, of God's wrath.

By 6:15, Farlanburg was in the middle of a lightning storm. Evelyn flung herself on the bed thinking that if a bolt struck her house and killed her, at least she wouldn't mash her face or bruise herself when she fell. Everybody had said how natural Leo looked at his funeral.

When the storm was over, she got up and went into the kitchen to fix herself a bite to eat. She didn't feel much like eating, but a body had to go on. She opened a can of chicken noodle soup, put it on the stove, and was thinking about all the unpacking she'd have to do. She stared out the window and spotted something on the road. The wind had knocked dead limbs from the trees and blown whatever was on the porch all over the yard. She decided to go have a look.

The downpour had stopped, but a fine mist blew through the valley. Rain had flattened the daffodils, and tiny rivers of brown water ran through the yard. The grass had never looked so green. Because of the storm, it was getting dark earlier than usual. Down near her poppy beds, Evelyn suddenly stopped. She was still several feet away when she knew. He lay on his side by the edge of the road, his fur a dark patch of butterscotch, rumpled and wet. She knelt and turned him over. There was no mark where the vehicle had struck him. Just blood where his nose and mouth touched the pavement and, under his hind legs, a small amount of waste that his bowels had released. His pink tongue was out as though he tasted something good.

Evelyn picked him up. He was still warm. She cradled him in her arms, threw her head back and tried to scream, but the only sound that came out of her was a weak, old-woman noise. She wasn't sure how long she sat there, but by the time she got up, the warmth had gone out of his body, and her legs felt as though they were being pricked by thousands of pins. His back parts went one way, his head and shoulders, another. She'd had no idea something dead could be so hard to carry.

She took him to the house and gently laid him in the rocking chair on the porch while she went to look for a box. She found an old boot box of Leo's in the hall closet and arranged the cat's body in a curved, sleeping position. She tucked one of Leo's sweaters in around him, then placed the box in the kitchen next to the water dish. Whatever needed doing would have to wait until morning.

She went to bed early, but couldn't sleep. She lay there listening for scratching noises, the scrape of claws on cardboard boxes, meows from dark corners. Sometime after midnight, she drifted off. She hadn't been asleep long when Leo came to her as silently as a cat and as quick on his feet. She couldn't see him but felt his presence, could hear the air rushing like wind through the tunnel of his nose. "Here kitty kitty," he called.

"Don't," Evelyn whimpered.

"So you want to take a trip," she heard him say. She couldn't pinpoint his location. "Why don't you come with me?" he said. Suddenly, he began to speak in a high-pitched, feminine voice. Whining. Mocking. "Oh Leo, I wish we could go to Florida," he said. "Oh Leo, I'd give anything to see my cousins in Cincinnati." He laughed and his laughter filled the room. "Come on," he said, groping for her. "I've come to take you with me. We're gonna start with a little trip to the garage and have a look at that left front tire. I'd swear I saw cat hairs between the tread."

His cold hands were pulling on her ankles, dragging her into a hole at the foot of the bed, when she woke up screaming. She began to cry, silently at first, biting the edge of the covers, then to sob as though she couldn't stop. "Leo," she whispered, her eyes searching the dark. "I'm afraid."

She lay there, remembering a time when she was six or seven and terrified to get up at night to pee. She had called for Jean, who'd slept across the room, had listened in agony to Jean's breathing, sleep sounds as soft as mattress feathers. She could never remember what she'd been afraid of—only that whatever it was eventually seemed less threatening than the restrictions it placed on her.

She threw off the covers and turned on the lamp. "Leo?" she whispered.

He was quiet.

"Leo?" she repeated. She got out of bed, stumbled down the hall, and switched on the light in the garage. She hurried to the left side of the car, got down on her knees, and was about to run her fingers around the tire when she suddenly stopped. She shook her head slightly and felt as if she were waking a second time but from a much longer dream. "No!" she said, jerking her hands back. "I couldn't have done that." She sat there a moment, letting her words soak in, and it occurred to her that she knew something about herself that

Leo, despite his claim of insight and the years he'd lived with her, had not known.

She got up slowly and began to walk toward her bedroom. When she yanked open the closet door, the smell of him flew out at her. She watched a flannel shirt slide from its hanger and fall to the floor. She stood there staring at it, then, without warning, her hand snatched a vest. She began to pull pants, shirts, and ties from their hangers and throw them in a pile at her feet. Suits, windbreakers, belts, socks and underwear from the drawers, shoes from his shoebag in the hall closet. She worked up a sweat. Gathering as much as she could carry, she ran to the front porch and flung everything on the steps. She went back for more, making several trips. When she finished, she ran down the porch steps and out into the yard. A cool wind ruffled her hair and played with the hem of her gown. She cupped her hands around her mouth. "Leo!" she cried. Her voice echoed from one hilltop to another. "You're dead," she yelled, "you son of a bitch!" She listened, watching the trees sway and nod against a background of dark sky. After awhile, she turned and went inside.

She buried them the next morning at dawn. Dug a little hole for Orville between the poppy beds and the box elder; dumped Leo's rain-soaked belongings in the garbage cans. When she finished, she showered, put on a yellow pantsuit, and drove into town. She stopped at the florist's and bought herself a corsage.

There was a small crowd waiting in front of the bus when she got there. In line ahead of her stood Francine Settles, Dora Haynes, and a lot of other people from Evelyn's church. Francine and Dora, both widowed, had arranged to be partners for the trip. Dora was trying to explain to Francine that by sharing a room with her, she had saved Francine a total of fifteen dollars. She clutched her big, black purse to her body and pointed her finger at Francine as if it were a revolver. "Any way you look at it, you owe me," she said. "You can buy my dinner, or I'll be glad to pick out something at one of the souvenir shops, but I don't think it's right that you try to weasel out of it. If it hadn't been for me, you'd be paying full fare."

Francine turned to the woman behind her and remarked that nothing disillusioned her so much as discovering greed in the heart of a fellow member of her Sunday school class.

Mrs. Garland Hornby stood next to the bus door, crossing off names, and telling everyone how nice they looked. "Why, Evelyn!" she said, "You look like the essence of spring." With her pen, she touched the corsage on Evelyn's chest. "And what a lovely, lovely flower."

"Thank you," said Evelyn. As she boarded the bus, she turned and looked over her shoulder. "It's an orchid," she said, "in case you didn't know."

Maude Simpson and her husband Hayward sat opposite Evelyn, across the aisle. Hayward, who farmed, slumped in his seat next to the window and sulked like a man who'd rather be home vaccinating steers. Maude waited until Evelyn got situated, then leaned over and gave Evelyn's shoulder a little squeeze. "I know this has been just an *awful* year for you," she said. "How are you doing?"

Evelyn expected her mouth to spill the whole story, but it did not. She searched for a mournful expression to match Maude's and was surprised that she couldn't find one. She glanced at Hayward, watched him drum his thick fingers on the seat. "Better," she said, and for the first time in more than forty years, she meant it.

Ollie's
Gate

Ollie Ellyson was the only woman I knew during my growing-up years who sounded like she was telling the truth when she said she *liked* men. This made her seem wicked and exotic. At the same time, I thought of her as saintly because it seemed to me she had every reason to hate them.

She lived with her brother Crater at their homeplace a little more than a mile from where we lived. They were both old when I knew them, but I didn't think of them that way. To me they were just Crater and Ollie—same as they'd always been.

Our families went way back, further back than I can remember, in a way that only people who sleep in the same houses their grandparents were born in can do. We went as far back as my mother and my mother's mother, who used to play with Crater and Ollie when she was a girl. We passed them down from one generation to another, so my memories of them are somewhat like stray dogs in that I don't always know who owns them.

This one is mine. It was winter. January. I was nine and spending the night with Ollie. Outside, the snow swirled and drifted and white flakes flew at the windows like things that wanted in. I was warm in Ollie's bed under covers that smelled like company and mothballs.

Down the hall, Crater sat slumped in his chair, his sweater pulled up around his ears. I couldn't see him, but I could picture him alone in the dark. He looked up now and then as a voice, Ollie's or mine, moved like a shadow past the door to his room.

Ollie stood near the hearth, nightgown hiked up, warming her bare behind. The cheeks of her rear end were orange in the firelight and dimpled like pumpkins that have seen too many frosts. The floor creaked as she shifted her weight and talked about men.

"I've done my share of wanting them," she said. "Used to love to be in the company of men. Some women are that way, Leafy Lee."

I listened to her words and let them take their place within me. I'd grown up hearing her.

"I don't know why I talk to you like this," she said, nibbling at a fingernail. "You're too little to understand."

"I do understand!" I told her. "Really I do. Just ask me. About the wanting part or any of it. I've had the wants a lot, myself, since I turned nine."

Ollie cackled, a dry, wicked-old-woman sound, like wind blowing brown winter leaves. "This is a pity," she said.

"What is?"

"I'm telling you things you'll need to know one day, and

you won't even be able to remember them."

"You can tell me all over again."

She shook her head, pulled at the turtle-skin textured folds of flesh on her neck. "I'm old, sugarpie. I may not be around to tell you."

I stared at her, then looked around the room. Normally Ollie slept upstairs. There wasn't much heat up there in the winter, and when I spent the night with her, she pulled a hide-a-bed from the worn, velvety couch in the parlor. I knew the full name of every solemn-faced, white-eyed Ellyson ancestor whose picture hung there. I'd laid claim to my favorite wall tapestries, knew which figurines had been broken and had heads held on with glue. I had come to think of Ollie's parlor as my room. It had never occurred to me that my nights in her house might end. A sudden gust of cold wind caused the curtains behind the couch to lift slightly, and I pulled the covers higher around my neck and burrowed in.

She lowered her head, moved a sock-covered foot in little circles tracing flower patterns in her rug. "I know you can't remember everything we talk about, but try to remember this. Don't waste your wanting years, Leafy Lee. When you get a little older, old enough to do some real wanting of your own, don't let anyone tell you what you're feeling isn't right. You know when you're hungry. Don't listen to them what's lost their appetite." She closed her eyes and began to twist a section of frizzy white hair. "Being with a man for the first time, if he's the right man, should be like sitting down to that first bowl of new potatoes and peas in early spring," she said. "You may have potatoes and peas twice a day after that, but if the first bowl was everything it should've been, nothing else'll ever quite measure up."

With that, she let go of the tail of her nightgown, and it fell like a curtain down over her legs. She turned out the light, got into bed, and patted my shoulder as she said good night. I lay there a long time listening to the logs pop and crackle in the fireplace and wondered what it felt like to be hungry for men. I closed my eyes, touched my stomach, and tried on the feeling. I imagined the sweet ache of it, a kind of craving. Like wanting mincemeat pies and knowing you won't get any till Christmas. Or hankering for just one bite of the homemade sausages Ollie kept in quart jars in her spider-infested cellar. I wanted to suggest a trip to the kitchen but decided against it. Polite kids do not go to other people's houses and beg for food.

Later, when the logs were mostly ashes and the ashes were losing their glow, I listened to the steady rhythm of her sleep beside me. "You aren't old," I said, putting my arm around her, remembering something I'd overheard Crater say to a visitor one Sunday afternoon. "Some women get too old for it," he said. "Then there are those like Ollie who never do."

Crater and Ollie were the only people I ever knew who drank coffee by dipping it up with a spoon. They did their dipping out of some of the same cups and in some of the same rooms as their great-grandfather had more than one hundred years before. I think they knew by the number of buckets Ollie carried upstairs during a rainstorm that they would be the last to live there. They were the missing pieces to what had once been a twelve-piece set. A mother, father, and several brothers waited for them under the cedars on the hill behind the house.

Crater and Ollie's house was the kind of place I liked to go to. A place where everything stayed the same. The red poppies had come up in the round beds in the front yard as long as I could remember, and the arrangement of the wicker chairs on the sagging, vine-shaded porches was as permanent as the wrinkles on Crater's and Ollie's faces. It was a place where people told me things, grown-up kinds of things that others hid behind whispers. A place where I could be too young and no one would hold it against me.

I was too young to go there. That's what my mother told me the year I started sixth grade. She had said nothing about my being too young the year before when I was in the fifth. Not a word during the years before that. I have a disease, I thought, and no one has told me. My life has gone as far forward as it can, now I'm moving in reverse. My friends will go on through junior high and grow up, and I will get younger and younger each year until I cease to exist.

"Why don't you want me to go there anymore?" I asked my mother one evening. She was at the lower end of the yard picking Japanese beetles off her dahlias and dropping them into quart jars filled with kerosene. It was mid-September. The leaves on the maple tree in our front yard were a tired shade of green; the sky, an endless blue like looking straight into the eyes of God.

My mother was a tall, thin-lipped woman. Efficient is the word that comes to mind. She waited until one hand was filled with beetles, then squatted and watched them avalanche through the mouth of the jar.

I was pretty sure she'd been young once, maybe even a little fun-loving. At least she looked that way in the high school graduation picture she kept in her sock and brassiere drawer in her room. But by the time I came along, she had metamorphosed into a wife and a mother, and she moved through each day looking tired and vaguely disappointed with the life she had found in her cocoon. It was the same with most of the women I knew.

"I never said you couldn't go there," she replied, her hands hovering like bees over the flowers. "I just wish you'd spend more time with people your own age."

I sat down, plucked a dandelion, and planted it behind my ear. The evening sunlight warmed my skin and made me feel tropical. I pictured myself between the covers of the *National Geographics* we were allowed to look at during library hour at school. "But I like Crater and Ollie," I said.

My mother reached into a red, plastic bucket at her feet, took out a can, and began to dust the flowers with Sevin. "I like them, too, Leafy Lee. You know that."

"At least they're fun," I said. "At least they don't treat me like I'm a baby."

My mother put the Sevin back in the bucket and sighed. "Maybe I don't always treat you like you're grown up," she said, "but that's because you aren't. I'm your mother, and I want what's best for you. There are still things I'd like to protect you from."

"From Crater and Ollie?" I said, giving her one of my can't-you-see-what-an-old-sour-puss-you're-being kind of looks. But my look was wasted on her because she had already picked up her bucket and was heading toward the house.

"You just don't want me to go there!" I yelled. "You used to go there all the time when you were a kid. You had fun. You never want me to have fun or do any of the things you did." I pulled up another dandelion and ate it out of spite. I hope I get sick, I thought. I hope there are ants in this dandelion and they crawl around in my stomach and make tunnels and I die.

"It's Friday night," my mother called wearily over her shoulder. "Come inside and I'll let you help me bake a spice cake for your Daddy. He'll be home in a little bit." My father worked at a factory in Ohio and only came home on weekends. Although he always had a cake waiting for him on the dining room table, it was cold and tasted to me like it had been baked more out of duty than love. I was surprised he couldn't tell the difference.

I snatched the dandelion from behind my ear, threw it as hard as I could, and watched it land in the grass. I wanted to stay there in the yard to show my mother I was growing up and would not be treated like a baby. The dandelion I had swallowed was now a sour burn in my stomach. If I'm going to die, I thought, let it be here in her yard. Let the grass grow extra tall around me and let her not find me until spring when she runs over me with the lawnmower and my bones clog the blades. But she was baking a cake, and I liked to lick the beaters. I got up and went inside.

I knew she'd changed the subject as she'd been doing lately every time we talked about Crater and Ollie. And in the kitchen, I caught her looking at me in a strange way while I greased and floured the cake pans. She stared at me a lot that fall, and there was something new in it. Like she was checking for changes. Like she expected not to know me.

"What do you and Ollie talk about?" she asked me every few days. She tried to make it sound like a casual question. Tried to make it sound the same as "Who got in trouble on the bus today?" or "What did you have for lunch at school, Leafy Lee?" But I heard a difference in the level of interest behind the asking.

"Nothing much," I said the first time she questioned me. "Peonies," I told her the next time. "Ollie talks a lot about her peonies, and she's teaching me to make meringue on pies."

"Hmmmm," said my mother. "Doesn't sound like much fun to me."

I shrugged. I knew my mother had spent a lot of time at Ollie's house. Ollie had told me. And I wondered if Ollie had talked to her about the same things she discussed with me. I suspected that my mother had once been fascinated by Ollie, drawn to her in a way she didn't understand, just as I was. We never discussed the reason for that fascination but kept it like a thought on layaway between us.

It couldn't have been Ollie's beauty. The dark-haired girl with the dimple in her chin whose picture hung in Ollie's upstairs hallway was like a guest who had stayed only a short while and then gone, long before my mother or I had the chance to know her. In her place was *our* Ollie, the familiar one, with several chins instead of one that was dimpled and with hair that had mutinied, gone wild and white.

Whatever drew us to her had nothing to do with things that fade. It was something I couldn't see or explain except to say that I felt strong when I was around her, capable of handling any troubles, any terrible disappointments that crouched and waited for me in the years ahead. Those things were real, I knew, and happened to people when they grew up. A bad thing had happened to Ollie. I heard grown-ups talking about it when they thought I wasn't listening.

Most of what I heard came from old women. Brittle-boned, sour-smelling "girls" with names like Ruth or Imogene or Ella. They'd been friends with my grandmother, and they still dropped by once each summer, accompanied by middle-aged sons and daughters who rattled change in their pockets, swatted at flies or stood out in the yard and took pictures of ordinary hills.

The old women always headed for soft chairs in our living room. They encouraged me to prowl through their purses for chewing gum, let me smell the perfumed corsages that bobbled above their shrunken breasts. I was more interested in listening to their heartbeats, but my mother glared at me until I left them alone. I wouldn't have been surprised to put my ear there and find any one of them dead.

They came to reminisce, eat our cookies, and talk about sin. Sin would ruin your life, they said. Turn your mouth upside down, your soul inside out, crush you until you were sorry. Ollie was a sinner, they said, which was why God had denied her what a woman wants most out of life—a husband and family of her own. When they talked about her, their faded eyes grew bright, almost glittered. I used to wonder if they would've been as interested in discussing Ollie if she'd been dead. I could've sworn they felt cheated because her sins hadn't killed her.

"How come you never had a husband?" I asked Ollie once, not long after my dead grandmother's friends had paid us a visit.

Ollie didn't say anything for a while but gave me one of her looks that let me know I'd repeated something stupid. "Just because I've come home empty-handed, doesn't mean I haven't been to the store," she said.

During all the years I knew her, she seldom discussed her life with me. Usually, we discussed her ideas. I guess she figured I already knew those things about her most people thought were worth knowing. I did, and what I didn't learn from my grandmother's friends, I learned from Crater.

Some people don't like illegitimate babies. Crater was one of those people. He especially disliked the thought of one calling him "Uncle." I used to think if he'd lived in a town big enough to have a Holiday Inn or a murder once in a while on the streets, he might not have been so dead set against the babies. But the nearest town was Farlanburg, the county seat, and Crater carried on over a little thing like an illegitimate baby more than any man I've ever known. Ollie had one once, and she wasn't sorry. It was never clear to me which of the two things Crater couldn't forgive her for.

I can't remember ever not knowing about Ollie's baby. I was half-grown before I found out that the "bad" thing that had happened to Ollie was something I already knew. I must have carried words like "bastard" and "whore" around with me since birth. When you're young, the sound of the words is all that matters. They have no meaning. As you grow older, the words begin to follow you around like annoying friends. They knock and want to explain themselves. They wait for the day that you will let them in.

I remember Crater's first words to me about Ollie. "Count your blessings, Leafy Lee, that you ain't pretty. Beauty in a woman is a curse," he said before I was old enough to get his drift. It was his way, in the early days, of trying to influence my opinion of Ollie. But to me, it was nothing more than a clue that there are some things even parents are too kind to tell their kids.

We were sitting on the porch together one afternoon cracking hickory nuts for one of Ollie's pies. I was in the third grade—old enough to want to know it all, young enough to think I'd understand. Zeb and Carrie Jean, Crater's foxhounds, were frolicking with a black dog in the weeds just beyond the yard fence. Crater had ordered his hounds from a breeder in the southern part of the state, near Beckley. Although he'd never said how much he'd paid for them, I'd heard him brag enough to know that it was plenty. The black dog was trying to stand on Carrie Jean's back as if he wanted to raise himself above his surroundings to have a better view of the world.

"Look what someone's trained that dog to do!" I shouted, pointing at the act. "I bet that dog has run away from a circus somewhere."

Crater began to cuss and wave his cane wildly. He grabbed a handful of hickory nuts and hurled them toward the fence. By the time he was able to get out of his chair and down the steps, the ruckus between the dogs was finished. Crater's anger was not. He stood in the yard trembling, his elbows hiking up behind him. "Bitch!" he yelled, spit flying from his mouth. I thought he was having some kind of fit. "Carrie Jean, you bitch!" he yelled again, and I was a little afraid of him.

He turned and saw me looking at him. I had slipped out of my chair and was crouched behind it. "That dog'll take up with anything," he said as he huffed and puffed his way up the steps. "I've always said there ain't a lot of difference between dogs in heat and some women. That one reminds me a lot of your friend Ollie."

He half-fell into his rocking chair, and when I saw that he meant me no harm, I went back to cracking nuts. We didn't say anything. After a while, he cleared his throat, and when I looked up, he was squinting at me. "What d'you think them dogs was doing?" he growled.

"Don't know. Playing, I reckon."

Crater grunted. "Playing hell. Them dogs was making pups."

I didn't understand why dogs making pups had made Crater so angry or why he had put all the blame on Carrie Jean. I wasn't about to ask. That evening, I headed up the hollow but stopped a short distance above the house. I watched until Crater got up and went inside, then I crept back down the road and crawled around in the weeds just beyond the yard fence. "Big liar," I said later as I kicked rocks on my way home. I had searched every inch of those weeds, had surprised two lizards, and found a snake skin, but not a single pup.

Crater and Ollie had quarreled for as long as I could remember. The silence between them had grown as steadily as the grass over the stones in their walk. By the time I knew them, they quarreled at, rather than with, each other because they hadn't spoken in more than thirty years. I visited them in spite of the quarreling. Maybe a little because of it.

They gave me messages to carry. Important things like: "You tell him if he doesn't want stiff underwear, he can pay someone in town to wash them, and I won't have to freeze to death hanging them on the line."

"You tell her I'll get my sheep out of her flower beds when I'm good and ready. Sheep make money. Flowers don't."

I'm not sure how they managed when I wasn't around.

I used to imagine what their last conversation must have been like. I wondered if it played over and over like a record inside their heads. Crater sang his version of their trouble for company whenever company was handy. He'd sit on the front porch and say things about Ollie that would cause her to go upstairs without me and lock herself in her room.

I learned to hate his company. Maybe to keep from hating him. Company did things to Crater's mouth. It loosened his tongue and worked on him like a laxative causing secrets he carried inside him to bubble and rumble and finally slide out. They were not his secrets to tell. Besides, they were secrets most people already knew.

Ollie could tell ahead of time when he was going to do it. She talked of leaving him then, turning her back on him and the homeplace for good. On those days, I found her in the kitchen making pound cakes, sweet, buttery things the color of petals on a black-eyed susan. The smell of them clung to her dress for days. Ollie always baked pound cakes when she talked about leaving. She baked them, I think, to keep from going somewhere.

"He's in one of his moods again. Has himself in a lather," she said when I stopped by on my way home from school one day near the beginning of seventh grade. She was sitting on the back porch in her willow rocker, legs spread wide, breasts resting on her rib cage like two loaves of yeast bread. "Sometimes I wish for things I shouldn't wish for," she said. "Sometimes I wish something would happen to him. My own brother. Something that would close his trap and shut him up for good." She dabbed at her eyes with her apron and turned her face from me but not before I saw the tormented look that had settled there. It was as though she thought that wishing for Crater's death might make it happen.

She got up and went into the kitchen. I followed her. I put my lunchbox and books in a corner and hopped up on a stool. My mouth began to water as she creamed butter and sugar by hand in a bowl. "I've got almost twenty dollars in my money can," I said. "That doesn't count my stack of quarters. We could buy a gate and put it at the mouth of this hollow. One of those fancy jobs like you see in pictures of heaven or Hollywood. We could put a big lock on it. I'd like to see any company try to get through it then."

Ollie let go of her spoon and squinched up her face like she was about to cry. "What good do you think that'd do?" she said, turning her palms toward the ceiling and shaking her hands in front of my face. "It's not what's off this hollow that's giving me trouble." She picked up her spoon and began to stir frenziedly. "You can't always blame others when things are going wrong for you, Leafy Lee. We're the ones," she snapped. "Crater and me. This is between the two of us."

My eyes blurred. My mouth began to quiver. "Fine with me!" I said. "I was mistakenly impressionated that there were three of us. If you don't want my help, don't go telling me your problems." I picked up my lunchbox and books, stomped out of the kitchen, and let the door slam as I bounded down the porch steps. I was on the bottom step when I heard her begin to cry. It was a strange sound, I thought, for a human to make; more like an animal whining or an owl. I threw my books and lunchbox in the grass and ran back inside. She was sitting at the table, one hand over her eyes, the other loosely holding the wooden spoon from which something thick and yellow like egg dripped onto the floor.

I put my arms around her and told her I was sorry. She let go of the spoon and sat there with her arm as limp and straight as if it had been broken. I didn't know what to do. When her shoulders began to shake, I sat down at the table and cried, too.

After a while, I sniffed and wiped my nose on my sleeve. "You could come to my house and stay with me awhile," I said. I was afraid to say she could stay forever. My mother was not one to welcome friends home from school. I didn't know whether that included Ollie.

Ollie fished for her handkerchief in her apron pocket, pulled it out and wiped her eyes, then blew her nose. She smiled at me, leaned forward, and put her hand on my cheek. "It's not you, Leafy Lee," she said. "I don't want you thinking that. I just never thought the day'd come I'd even think about leaving this place. But I don't know how much more of him I can take."

After that, I was determined to hate Crater. I said more mean things behind his back that year than I did to Carlos Kemper's face. Carlos Kemper was a boy who rode the school bus with me. He had yellow bangs, teeth the same color, and he was shaped like a Hubbard squash. One of his favorite tricks was to get little kids to shut their eyes and stick out their tongues. "I have something good for you," Carlos would sing, then he'd spit into their mouths. It was easy to hate Carlos Kemper. Crater was another story.

I couldn't forget what Ollie'd said about wishing something would happen to Crater. For a while, I tried to think of ways to make her wish come true. I'd pick up sticks and rocks in the yard and slip around the house to the front porch where Crater sat. I never knew what I planned to do with my weapons. It didn't matter. I'd take one look at him, like what I saw, and forget what I'd come around there for. He wore baggy pants, a flannel shirt, and sweater. His long johns hung out from under his clothes like a second skin. He bundled himself up like that no matter what the season. His eyes were closed, his chest rose and fell as easily as a Sunday afternoon wind. It was hard to want to kill a man who looked like that.

"Sssstttt," he'd say, opening one eye and motioning for me to come closer. "Whose friend are you?" he'd whisper. When I was younger, he'd given me candy—round, pink stuff— from a sack he kept inside his sweater. I'd take the candy and hear him laughing and wheezing as I ran and hid behind the lilac bush where I'd hide and eat what he'd given me. As I got older, he gave me quarters. Afterwards, on my way home, I'd feel like a traitor, sick with guilt, heavy as Judas from the weight of the silver coins in my shoes.

There were times, if Ollie had gone up to the cemetery to clean graves or take fresh flowers, I would even sit on the porch and listen to his stories while we waited for his company to come. It did. You could sit on that porch on any Sunday in warm weather and wait for it to roll in. Crater was one of the oldest men around who still remembered things anyone wanted to hear, and there were some who would drag the mufflers off their Buicks and Chrysler LeBarons to get at him. They wanted him to tell them about the good old days. They wanted him to tell them about their great-grandparents and other great-people they never knew.

I remember an afternoon one year in April when I was in the ninth grade. Ollie had caught a ride to town. A man and a woman drove all the way from Parkersburg to see Crater. Genealogists, they called themselves, but their clothes were as bright as Easter eggs, and they looked like the type who wouldn't say no to a crucifixion.

The man patted Crater's liver-spotted hands and leaned close to shout questions into his hair-filled ears, while the woman watched the tape on her recorder go round and round. She looked up now and then and smiled at me, displaying a mouthful of teeth as pointy as the ends of spears.

Crater listened to them and nodded and looked out over his fields like a man who knows just when to plant. Planting was behind him, but that didn't matter. Where others saw thistles and iron weeds, Crater saw green growing corn.

"I've told you most of what I know," he said when he'd tired of their questions. He'd given them what they wanted: a country-size serving of local history spiced with just the right amount of gossip. Now he looked forward to dessert. "People back then were just about like they are now," he said. "Men worked harder. Women . . . what can I say about the women? Women don't change. Some were decent. Some decent enough. And even then we had our share of sluts. My sister,

Ollie, could tell you anything you want to know about the sluts."

Before she left, the genealogy woman asked if she could take my picture standing beside the corncrib with Crater's foxhounds. Though I was embarrassed, I let her. I didn't know how to say no to a woman from a city the size of Parkersburg. "Sit down here between the dogs and think of something sad," she said, and when I did, she aimed her camera at me, and I heard a click.

Afterwards, Crater and I sat on the porch and watched them drive away. "Well sir," Crater said, stretching his legs. "Think I'll mosey on up your way and see if there are any duck eggs along the creek."

"Why d'you do that?"

"What?"

"Talk about Ollie that way," I said. "Those people aren't genealogists. They're just blatherskites. Gatherers and spreaders. They were making fun of you." I was mad at him for what he'd said about Ollie and mad at myself, without knowing why, for letting the woman take my picture.

Crater popped a piece of candy in his mouth. "Well then, we all got something out of it," he said. "Besides, I didn't say nothing that wasn't true." He picked up his cane and looked out over his fields again. "Anyway, she deserves it."

"Who?"

"Her," he said, meaning Ollie.

"I'd like to know what she ever did to you?"

"She stole this family's reputation, is what she did," he snarled. His face turned purple. Weak-looking, old-man sweat dotted his forehead and neck. "There was a time, girlie, when the Ellyson name meant something in this community. A man could go into town 'thought having to worry that people were laughing behind his back."

I looked at Crater. For the first time, it occurred to me that other people might find him strange and think the same about Ollie. They might feel that way about all of us on the hollow. I had no idea who I meant by "other people," but whoever they were, I suddenly knew that we weren't like them, and I was embarrassed by the fact. If they find out about us, I thought, they will come in here in droves and gawk. They'll put our pictures in *National Geographic* alongside naked men and women and sun-baked babies who have rings in their noses and saucers sewn in their lips. They'll point and laugh at us during library hour, and we'll be known as "The People That Time Forgot."

"You haven't been to town in years!" I said, surprised by the anger in my voice. "I've been to town a million times since you have, and I've never heard anyone in town say anything about you and Ollie. People in town are busy. They've got better things to do."

It was true. It had to be. I decided then and there that I was going to live in town one day, myself. Town people were normal and modern, I knew. They didn't gossip or sit around chewing over the past. They didn't waste their Sundays visiting cemeteries or trying to chase sheep back through a hole in the fence.

Crater looked at me but didn't say anything. After awhile, I began to worry. I got out of my chair and sat down on the top porch step. "Shoot," I said, not quite as bold as I'd been a little earlier. I was afraid he'd tell my mother I'd sassed him. "What happened to Ollie wasn't all that bad. I could tell you some things that go on nowadays that'd curl your toenails." Truth was, I didn't know what went on nowadays or any other, but I saw no harm in pretending. If I joined in those kinds of conversations at school, what I said never sounded right. I figured Crater wouldn't know the difference. "Yeah,"

I bragged, "I could tell you some things that'd set your ears on fire."

Crater's jaw muscles tightened visibly. He looked at me coldly. "You speaking from experience, missy?"

I shook my head quickly and started to say something.

"Thought so," said Crater. "She's too old and ugly to have her own fun any more. Wait'll I tell your Mama how Ollie's made a Jezebel out of you."

Not long after that, my mother had her first and only conversation with me about sex. At least that's the way she remembered it in later years. I remember it more as a conversation about Ollie.

My mother asked me if I wanted to go for a walk with her one evening. We put on sweaters, strolled down the hollow. There was a paleness, a softness about her voice that matched the woods, which were light green and filling up with flowers. I hear that conversation every now and then when the leaves are new on the trees or when I discover a mayapple, jack-in-the-pulpit, or one of the other spring beauties pressed between the pages of a book.

As we walked, she kept her hands in her sweater pockets and commented on the abundance of wild onions in the field. Without warning, she suddenly asked me, "Leafy Lee, do you know how you got here?"

I looked at her face to see if she was joking. It would have been unlike her. "Walked, I reckon," I said.

Her face reddened and she shook her head quickly. "Not here, specifically. I mean do you know how you came into the world?"

"Please don't let her tell me something weird. Please let my beginning have been the same as everyone else's," I silently prayed. I tried to appear calm and answered my mother by rolling my eyes up in my head and reminding her that I was in the ninth grade. Although I didn't tell her, I had known about babies since the sixth. Carlos Kemper was as foulmouthed as he was ugly. He'd been allowed to watch everything that happens on a farm, and there was nothing he wouldn't gleefully explain to any kid on the bus. What details he didn't know, he made up.

I could sense my mother's relief. It hung in the air as heavy as wood smoke. But she wasn't finished. She wanted to talk to me about Ollie, she said. She folded her arms and sidestepped a mudhole as we continued walking. "Ollie made some mistakes," she said. "We all have. Everyone makes mistakes, Leafy Lee. It's just that some get noticed more than others."

I wondered why she was telling me this. I had already figured out that having babies was a mistake and had vowed never to have any. I braced myself for her confession that she was sorry she'd had me.

She stopped and picked a leaf of ground ivy and twiddled it with her fingers. "It's sort of like Ida Gordon when she sings off-key at church. As long as she's singing with the choir, no one notices. It's the solos that get her into trouble. Do you see what I mean?"

I nodded, but I saw nothing.

"Well, Ollie's a woman who's spent her life off key, and she's never had the security of a choir behind her," my mother said, looking uncomfortable. "What I'm trying to say is that she's always been different in a way most people consider unacceptable. Women are supposed to . . . there are certain things they're supposed to do with their lives."

I frowned at her.

"Marriage. A husband. Children," she said. She seemed annoyed by what she was saying and determined to take it out on me. "This might sound hard to you, Leafy Lee, but you soon learn that it doesn't matter much *who* you marry as long as you *do* marry. That doesn't have to mean you won't love your husband. You just come to realize you could've loved any of the local boys equally well."

I thought of Carlos Kemper and felt sick.

"Some women aren't like that," my mother continued. "They can love only one man, and they'll make fools of themselves, sacrifice everything—including their standing in the community—to have him." She bit into the ivy leaf, made a face, then tossed the leaf on the ground. "I'm not made that way, myself.

"Ollie was only eighteen years old when Holten Westfall came in here with one of the oil companies. He was from somewhere in Pennsylvania, your grandma said. He wasn't like the men around here. He talked city, and he smelled good. I guess Ollie liked that in a man.

"Before long, he was spending a lot of time at Ollie's house. And why not? She was the prettiest girl around. Ollie's mother was dead. It's a dangerous thing for a girl to be pretty without a mother. Soon, rumor had it that if you passed by the house around midnight, you'd see Holten Westfall climbing like a cat up the porch vines and into Ollie's window. When Ollie turned up pregnant, he climbed down in a hurry, and no one ever saw him around here again.

"Ollie went away to have the baby, and when she came home, she came empty-handed. Your grandma and Ollie had been best friends until then, but Grandma was a good, Christian woman. She and Ollie never had much to do with each other after that."

I walked over to the ditch, squatted and used my finger to stir tadpoles. "Did you ever feel the same way about Dad? Love him as much as Ollie loved Holten Westfall?"

My mother sighed. "Why do you want to know things like that?"

I looked at her but didn't answer.

"No," she said. "I don't suppose I ever did."

"Then why'd you marry him?"

"I don't know. Because he asked me, I guess."

That evening, as I lay in my bed thinking, I knew that a high forehead and a fondness for clean shoes were the only things my mother, grandmother, and I had ever had in common. I never asked Ollie about Holten Westfall. "People will tell you what they want you to know when they want you to know it," Ollie'd told me once, and I'd remembered it. When the time came that she finally did tell me what she wanted me to know, I regretted ever having heard it from anyone else.

She told me for the first and only time one afternoon when we were upstairs looking at pictures in her room. It was near the end of my sophomore year in high school. We didn't go to her room often, but when we did, I always got the feeling it hadn't changed much since she was nineteen. The roses in the wallpaper and curtains had faded to a pale, almost gray, shade of pink. The closets were filled with old hats and clothes—taffeta dresses that rustled as though blown by a secret wind.

I sat on the floor surrounded by yellowed photographs. I had looked at Ollie's photographs a hundred times before. "How old were you in this one?" I said, holding up a picture of Ollie and her brothers.

"Seventeen," she said. She pointed to a brother who had

his arm around her shoulders. "That's Crater." She took the picture from me, looked at it, and passed it back. She pulled up a chair, sat down, and took another photograph from the box. "July 1913," someone had written at the bottom. "A picnic," she said. "At the Chimney Rock on Herb Stinson's farm. We were playing tag that day, and Willis Moyers almost killed himself falling off a rock. Would've if the trees hadn't broken his fall. Fool," she said, laughing.

There were lots of pictures like that in the box; pictures that could make her laugh and make me remember people I'd never known. That was the fun of looking at photographs with Ollie. She had a way with time, could make dead people talk, put life in them again.

When I looked up, she was staring at another picture, and her smile was gone. I stood up and peeked over her shoulder. "My family," she said.

I'd seen the picture before but had never noticed something odd about it. "Where are you?"

She looked at me for a moment, her eyes searching my face. "I'm not in it."

"Why not?"

"Crater wouldn't have it," she said, carefully. "Something had happened by this time. Something that caused hard feelings between Crater and me."

"I know," I mumbled, pretending to look for something in the box.

"Of course you know. Most people do." Ollie put her hand on my shoulder. "You're getting to be a big girl, Leafy Lee. I don't know what all Crater's told you, but it's time you knew the truth."

What she told me was similar to what I'd heard from my mother. The difference was in *hearing* it from Ollie. The moment she began to talk about Holten Westfall, her face changed. It reminded me of the way she looked when she was in her kitchen and had just tasted something good.

"Oh my, but he was a sweet thing," she said. She smacked her lips, smiled, and ran her hands slowly down over her chest. "Wavy black hair. Blue eyes. The nicest hands. I think he had the nicest hands I've ever seen on a man." She didn't sigh or put on a bittersweet expression as I'd seen women do on TV when they talked about old lovers. There was nothing about her face to indicate she was remembering a time of her life that had brought her anything but joy.

"You may've heard he was married, but that's not true. But I bet there's been many a girl what's wished he would've asked them. I suppose I could've made him marry me like Crater wanted. Could've made him pay for what he'd done, but I don't think a man ever owes a woman that. He was the best thing that ever happened to me, Leafy Lee, and I don't want you to think bad of him. I loved him, and I've never really loved anyone else."

Her expression changed then as though something had left a sour taste in her mouth. "Things then weren't like they are now. I don't say that to excuse myself. I just want you to know how it was. I was young. My older brothers were married and had worries of their own. There was no one but Crater. I couldn't go to Dad.

"When I told Crater I was pregnant, he said he'd help me. 'I'll take you to Charleston,' he said. 'There's a place down there where you can have it. Then we'll give it away, to someone decent.' He said that afterward we'd both just forget the whole thing. Pretend it never happened. I listened to him. At the time, it seemed I had no other choice. When it was over, Crater wouldn't forget. He wouldn't let me forget. That baby has been with both of us every day of our lives since."

She got up slowly, and walked to the window where she pulled back the curtains and stood looking down at her yard. "I used to think I'd get my baby back again. There were no records then. Just a nod of the head, and you were done with it. I used to look for him in the face of every kid that set foot on this place. After awhile, I just stopped looking."

She turned and faced me, and neither of us said anything. I looked away, and when I looked back, she had already gone downstairs. I sat at her dressing table, drew circles in the dust on boxes of old powder, and stared at myself in her mirror. "I could've been a virgin again if Crater would only've let me," she'd said as she was going, and while I didn't understand at the time how that physically could happen, I now know that the possibility of it happening was not as important to her as having the freedom for it to.

She left on a Sunday toward the end of a summer. Even waited till Crater's company had come and gone. I never knew what triggered her leaving or whether anything out of the ordinary happened that day to make her go. "A house starts to rot years before the walls cave in," I once heard her say, and although I have taken her statement out of context, I think it may apply.

I had finished my senior year in high school and no longer seemed to have the time to visit Crater and Ollie as often as I used to. Maybe I stopped wanting to go there for the same reason I no longer ate dandelions or crawled around in the weeds looking for pups. It could have had something to do with Carlos Kemper's getting on the bus one morning and calling me a whore because I wouldn't go to a Future Farmers of America dance with him. "I'm no whore, you ugly, yellow-toothed idiot, and you know it," I told him.

"Maybe not," he sneered, "but my Mom says you're gonna be if you don't quit hanging out with that old woman who lives down below you."

I think I stopped going there for the same reason my mother did more than twenty-five years before me—I got tired of being part of a quarrel that seemed pointless and covered with dust. I guess I got old enough not to want to know it all, reached an age where I knew I was never going to understand.

The day Ollie left, she called my mother and said she wanted to see me. I had promised friends I would meet them in town that evening and was slightly perturbed at having to stop at Ollie's.

I found Crater sitting on the porch as usual. "Haven't seen you in a while," he said, looking out over his fields in that same old way that told me things with him were pretty much the same.

"Yeah," I said. "With graduation and getting ready for college, I've been pretty busy." I rattled my car keys to show that I was a woman on the move.

"Want some?" He opened his sweater and offered me some candy.

"Nah," I told him. "I gotta go to town, and I don't want that pink stuff all over my mouth."

He scratched around in his bag of goodies, then scooted his chair until he had his back to me. I shook my head, opened the screen door and went inside.

I checked the parlor. When I didn't find Ollie there, I headed for the kitchen. "Ollie?" I called.

"Up here!" she yelled back.

I think I knew as soon as I saw her standing at the top of

the stairs. She stood there looking down at me like an old queen, wearing one of those black taffeta dresses I used to see in her closet. She picked up her suitcase and came slowly down the stairs. At the bottom, she put her arms around me and said how could she not have noticed how tall I'd grown.

"Where you going?" I said, trying to make it sound like a casual question.

"Be happy for me, Leafy Lee."

"You're leaving, aren't you?" I said. I folded my arms and pretended to be interested in the pattern of the wallpaper in the hallway.

Ollie smiled.

"He shot off his mouth again, didn't he? Company came, and he thought he had to tell everything he knew. Old coot!"

Ollie shook her head. "Not that I know of," she said. "I was up at the cemetery visiting Mama and Dad while Crater's company was here. He could've let me have it with both barrels, and I wouldn't have known the difference."

"Well he must've done something!" I said, my eyes filling with tears. "Otherwise you wouldn't be leaving."

"He hasn't done a thing today he hasn't done for the past fifty years, Leafy Lee." Ollie moved her hand up and down the banister, her gnarled fingers picking at bumps in the layers of dark varnish.

"It's my fault," I said. "You wouldn't be going if I'd been here. I should've been here to carry those messages back and forth between you like I used to."

"Ssssshhhh," she said, patting my shoulder the way she used to when she said good night. "Remember the time I told you you can't always blame others when things are going wrong for you?"

I nodded.

"Well, I forgot to tell you that neither should you always blame you." She hugged me once more. "Now open that gate," she said, picking up her suitcase and smiling.

"What gate?" I said.

"The one I built for myself a long time ago at the mouth of this hollow. Open it wide, Leafy Lee, cause Ollie's coming through."

She sold some timber on a tract that had been deeded just to her and moved into a trailer next to a distant cousin's house about an hour's drive from home. The trailer was a dumpy thing, a silver box with a blue stripe at the top and a tank of propane that hung like a lung on the back. Not at all the kind of place I thought a woman like Ollie should live.

I visited her as often as I could whenever I was home from college. She always asked about Crater and how her flowers were doing in the homeplace yard.

"Crater's fine and as much of an old coot as ever," I told her. "He closes off most of the house in the winter and spends a lot of time in his room."

I never got around to telling her about the flowers. Not long after Ollie'd left, Eloise Davis asked Crater if he minded if she dug up some of Ollie's bulbs and transplanted them to her own yard.

"What the hell," Crater told me later. "What do a bunch of flowers mean to me?"

The last time I saw Ollie was during the Christmas holidays one year. I was out of college, had gone north, and was living in a city. It was true the people there didn't spend their Sundays visiting cemeteries or chasing sheep. Instead, they washed and waxed their cars, watered their lawns, and went to shopping malls. It was not at all the glamorous life I had expected. And gossip, I had learned, was peculiar to no certain locale. People are people, wherever they are.

I came home once a year to visit. When Ollie asked me why she didn't see me more often, I told her I didn't get much time off. It was partly true. What I didn't think I had the right to tell her was that it hurt to come home because the hollow wasn't the same without her. Nothing was the same anymore.

My father had stopped coming home at all. Although he stayed married to my mother, his spice cakes were baked by a woman in Ohio, I heard. In a strange way, I was happy for him and hoped that with each bite, he tasted love.

My mother was the only one whose life seemed not to have changed much. She attended church on Wednesday nights and Sundays, hoed in her garden, and went through several gallons of kerosene each summer. And if my father ever meant anything more to her than the Japanese beetles she held in her hand, she never said anything about it to me. She had married, produced a child, raised that child, and cooked for her husband. She had done her duty. Doing her duty hadn't made her happy, but she continued to wear her wedding ring.

Ollie and I spent our last afternoon together looking at old pictures like we used to, except she lay in her bed with me piled on it beside her. "Got any boyfriends?" she asked me.

"A couple," I said.

"Anything serious?" she wanted to know.

"Never," I told her. Marriage, I had decided, was not for me.

Ollie was quiet a moment, then I saw the familiar wicked-old-woman gleam in her eyes. "Well?" she said, poking me in the ribs.

I laughed. "Like sitting down to that first bowl of new potatoes and peas in early spring," I replied. And if it was a lie, it was the most gratifying one I've ever told because it made her laugh, cackle in a way I hadn't heard in years.

When it came time for me to leave, she insisted on walking me to the door. She tottered along beside me. "There are so many things I should've told you," she said, smiling at me with eyes that were filled with tears. "You're not a kid anymore, but I think you'd still understand."

I hugged her, promised to come back next year for a visit, and left before she had me sitting at her kitchen table crying, too.

On my way home, I stopped the car in front of Ollie's homeplace. Crater still lived there, but he didn't want company anymore. I got out and walked up to the fence. The yard was a tangle of sumac and blackberry briars.

A piece of curtain waved from a dark window on the second floor. Ollie's room. I knew the glass had been broken by some skinny-armed kid who had howled and thrown a rock to show off for his friends one night. But a part of me wanted to believe that it had been shattered by something trapped too long within.

As I stood there in the growing darkness with the first snow of the season falling in silent, slow motion around me, I mourned for Crater and Ollie and for what we all had lost. I never knew how much a leaving could change things. Tear the fabric of the way things used to be. People who leave take a lot more with them than a suitcase. That's the way it was with Ollie.

The
Druther
Stage

Saturdays were made for singing,"
says Louisa Nell. She runs around Buel's living room without
shoes. "The song of love is a say-ad song," she croons. It's
one of her favorites. She plugs in her tape recorder and steps
over a tangle of wires. In a corner, a black amplifier hunkers
and hums and blinks its red eyes. An umbilical-like cord con-
nects the amplifier to an acoustic guitar, which Louisa Nell
has placed, as carefully as she might a baby, in the recliner.
She takes a soft white cloth from her purse and wipes the
guitar's strings, unlatches a case, extracts an autoharp, and
props it against the magazine rack where it sits like a row of
teeth.

"Testing. Testing." She caresses the neck of the chrome-
plated mike for which she has just shelled out fifty-five dollars. OK. So she paid ninety. But she's not going to tell her

husband Nippy that. Nippy is a driller for the Equitable Gas Company, and he spends his days wallowing in well mud. He drives a big green truck and carries enough grease under his fingernails to silence a squeaky axle. "Woman, you spend too much," he growls. He forces her to lie.

Louisa Nell puts comfort ahead of appearance when she works. The hems of her plaid pants are rolled to mid-calf because loose threads tickle her ankles. She stops, hands on hips, and surveys the room. As she lifts the mike onto the stage, a raised plywood platform that sits where the television used to be, her bracelets jingle like tambourines. She could swear the floor vibrates, that a current runs through her. Rubbing her hands together, she hollers at Delphine: "Go round up your girls. I'm ready to sing."

For the past two years, Louisa Nell has spent every Saturday afternoon at her brother Buel's house teaching his girls how to sing. At forty-five, she hasn't given up hope of getting what she wanted most from life—a recording contract—but she's decided to devote a little of her talent to helping others. Charity beings at home, she figures. She's going to make stars of her nieces.

She plucks a wad of gum from her mouth and mashes it in Buel's ashtray. She doesn't see much of Buel because he builds cars at a factory in Ohio during the week; he comes home and tinkers with his Pontiac on weekends. Drives two hundred and fifty miles to lie on his back in the cockleburs behind the barn and let oil drip on his face all day Saturday. Lies on Delphine, his wife, on Saturday night. Fool, thinks Louisa Nell. If he had any sense, he'd stay in Cleveland and get overtime. Save up his money and try to make something of himself.

"Car-o-line? San-dra?" she calls sweetly. "Delphine, where

are those girls!" She pads down the hall to the dining room but finds no one. She sniffs. Homemade doughnuts or butter-scotch pies? Hard to tell which. Delphine's pie safe is always full. Delphine is just a country girl without talent. She cooks to make up for it, thinks Louisa Nell.

Louisa Nell is about to inspect the pie safe when she looks out the window and spies the tops of her nieces' heads bobbing past the bushes at the lower end of the yard. Delphine is right behind them with a switch. Those girls! Almost as big as their mother. They'll need new costumes before long.

Louisa Nell makes every stitch they wear on stage. She wants them to look professional. She has a fabric shop in what used to be her garage, and she sells material cheap. She got into the fabric business because she couldn't find accessories and notions for her nieces' costumes. Now she can order whatever she wants from her catalogs. "Try Finding a Sequin Anywhere Else in Farlanburg!" her weekly ad in the newspaper says. Nippy says the ad sounds condescending. "Stick to your gas wells," she tells him, but she secretly wonders where he learned such a big word.

A screen door squeaks, then slams. Caroline and Sandra saunter in and flop down on the couch. It's August, and the girls are sweating. Louisa Nell can feel their heat. "Let's get with it," she says.

"I want a Coke," says Caroline, the eldest.

"Wait," Louisa Nell rapid-fires, but Caroline is already half-way to the kitchen. Lately, Caroline has been pushing. Trying to see what she can get away with. Her moods are as ugly and unpredictable as the breakouts on her chin. She's an all-right looking girl, Louisa Nell supposes. Some have mistakenly called her pretty, but Louisa Nell wouldn't go that far. Caroline has straight hair, knobby knees, and bird legs—defects she inherited from her mother. Both girls took after Delphine instead of the Fitzwaters, which is what Louisa Nell was before she married and what she would've stayed, she thinks, if she'd had good sense.

Louisa Nell makes a funny face and sticks her tongue out at Caroline's back, then winks at Sandra, who is ten. Sandra puts her hand over her mouth and giggles. She's a skinny kid with teeth that slant backwards as though they've been kicked in toward her throat. Louisa Nell cannot explain it, but she feels a special bond with that child. She's the kind of kid Louisa Nell can't help but like. "You're my favorite," she tells Sandra every now and then. When she likes someone, she likes them. She read somewhere that it's not healthy for people to hide their true feelings. "Hiding one's true feelings can give one ulcers and premature heart attacks," the article said, or something like that. So she's not going to go around feeling guilty because she happens to like one niece best. She's even thought that if Buel's house ever caught fire while she was there, and she had time to save only one person besides herself, that person would be Sandra. There's a limit to what one woman can do.

Sandra does have one annoying habit, but it doesn't bother Louisa Nell to the extent she'd like to see the kid charred. Sandra rubs one foot against her ankle when she's nervous or embarrassed, which is what she is most of the time. She's doing it now. It makes her look like a locust. Like she's trying to climb out of herself.

"Quit that!" Louisa Nell tells her, and she reaches out and clamps onto Sandra's bare foot. Sandra grins. Louisa Nell smiles at her: a sweet girl even if she is awkward. Caroline's worse. No poise. No presence. Last time they performed was at the county 4-H Roundup. They got so scared she thought they were going to topple off the stage. They swallowed like they had molasses in their throats and held hands through the entire act. Terrified. Big girls like that. "You two keep holding on to each other that way, people's gonna think there's something wrong with you," she told them.

But they won. They always do. They're half Fitzwater, and they've got music in them. It's less than two weeks till the regional competition, and Louisa Nell doesn't intend to stop there. She's going all the way to state. They'll do it, by damn, or else.

Louisa Nell has a good voice herself, but a face no one wants to look at. Nippy broke the news. "Emmylou Harris you ain't," he said one night at supper when he found out she'd gone to Pittsburgh and dropped $300 to sit in a recording studio and have a demo tape made. Telling her the truth was the least he could do, he said, being her husband.

"You talking about my looks or my singing?" she said calmly.

"Both," he replied.

"Clod!" she screamed at him. "Shows what you know about the business. No one ever said being a damn prom queen was a prerequisition to singing." She gave a little shove with her foot, and her chair flew back from the table. "You think you know everything, but you don't. You wouldn't recognize potential if you had any. Who was it said that well they drilled on Lib Hinzman's place wouldn't give her gas to cook with, let alone heat her house. Try telling her that each month when she cashes that fat royalty check." She snatched her fork and her turkey potpie and stormed into the kitchen. "Some judge you are," she said, tossing the words over her shoulder as she went.

That night, after Nippy went to sleep, Louisa Nell lay in bed beside him, her husband of twenty-six years, and reacquainted herself with the landscape of his face. His nose stuck up like a drilling rig. His mouth, without his teeth, was as sunken as a sediment pit. She leaned over, put her lips next to his red, weather-beaten ear. "You ain't so hot yourself, mister," she said.

Saying it made her feel better, but she still couldn't sleep. She kept wondering whether Nippy had really meant what he said or whether he was just ticked off that she'd spent so much. The thing that really got to her, the thing that just burned her up, was that he had the nerve to act like he was doing her a favor by trying to discourage her. Secretly, he probably wanted to be a race car driver himself or at least own his own garage. Instead, he was just a driller for the Equitable Gas Company, and the fact depressed him. He wanted her to be depressed, too. There are people like that in the world, she reminded herself. People who, when they get cancer or divorced, cross their fingers and hope the same will happen to you.

She gave a quick jerk on the quilt and most of what had covered Nippy came sailing over to her side. She looked at him lying there in the moonlight, snoring contentedly, naked except for his boxer shorts. She wanted to shake him, wake him from his sleep. "There's a whole dimension called ambition's been left out of you!" she wanted to inform him, but she knew she'd just wind up wasting time having to explain what she meant. What the hell, she told herself. She'd turn it around. Use the experience to her advantage. Who knows. She might even write a song about it. Something in a minor key. She'd call her song, "Why Is It That The One Who Should Love You Best, Treats You Worst."

A lesser woman might have been discouraged. Louisa Nell is not. Persistence pays in her business, she knows, and she is prepared to persist. In addition to her own career and managing the careers of her nieces, she tries to make time for community service. She sings every Sunday at the Rocky Branch church and helped organize County Chorus. She sings the "Star-Spangled Banner" at all of Farlanburg High's home football games and has done so, without pay, for seven years. She's as much a fixture at the games as the goalposts.

And each year at the Farlanburg Folk Festival, she climbs on the back of a flatbed truck and belts out tune after tune. When she was younger, she won a few contests. Got paid now and then for an evening of song. Now she plays the Folk Festival. Free. Her music fills the streets, do-si-dos with the aroma of Lion's Club hotdogs and cotton candy. She's a home-town girl. She has a following.

She sings to former classmates, those sleepy-eyed boys and girls whose Future Ambition in the yearbook said, "Military. Pipeline. Undecided." They voted her most likely to succeed, and to them, she has. She is swamped with requests to give music lessons. Everytime she sings at a local jamboree, she gives autographs in the grocery store for the next six weeks.

But there are days when an unpleasant thought skulks at the back of her mind. Sometimes she thinks they trapped her, these former classmates. Is it possible, she wonders, to be limited by the smallness of someone else's dream?

When Caroline returns, Louisa Nell folds her arms and glares at her until Caroline sets her Coke on the coffee table. The girls know they're not allowed to eat or drink before they sing. It puts a rasp in their voices.

Louisa Nell points to the new mike and smiles. "Well? What do you think?"

"Neato!" says Sandra.

Caroline rolls her eyes up in her head.

Louisa Nell regards Caroline a moment. "No need to be unpleasant," she says. She turns to Sandra. "Cost me two hundred dollars. I had to drive all the way to Charleston to get it. The man who sold it to me said it used to belong to a gospel quartet. They're on the verge of being famous. A record's in the works." She chews on her lower lip. "He wouldn't say who they are."

"Wow!" says Sandra, bug-eyed.

"I woulda got a new one, but I figured, hey, this one will be a collector's item one of these days." Louisa Nell smiles. She steps up on the stage and strokes the mike. She'd hoped the girls would be pleased with it. She would have appreciated a little fuss. But no. Like most young people these days, they've been given too much. They've been using a Mr. Mike she ordered for them from WDTV. Should've let them keep it, she thinks, but it reeked of amateurism, which is the one thing, besides Nippy, Louisa Nell cannot abide.

She blows into the mike to remove foreign particles, then rubs the neck with her guitar-cleaning cloth. Religious or not, people still have germs. "Let's get this show on the road," she says. She sidles up to the mike, raises an eyebrow and puts her mouth so close to the head it looks like she's going to take a bite. "Hello all you folks out there in radio land!" she says. She jumps back, looks astonished, and points to herself as if to say, "Who, me?" It's all part of the act. She only does it to put the girls at ease. But something like a current passes through her again, and she's aware of a tingling sensation up and down her spine. She's not sure whether it's time to see the chiropractor or whether her equipment is shorting out.

"Can you hear me?" she asks. She adjusts the volume until her voice blares. Her words roll like summer thunder.

Sandra rubs her foot against her ankle and looks at Caroline.

"Yoo-hoo. Hel-looo," sings Louisa Nell. She taps the head of the mike, and the result is a loud, thumping sound as though someone is taking a beating. All this for Caroline, who sits at one end of the couch, hugs a cushion to her chest, and stares at the floor.

Caroline has problems, chief among them her attitude. She's just coming into what Louisa Nell refers to as the "druther" stage. "Bwess its heart," says Louisa Nell. She looks at Caroline. "It'd druther be out in the bushes chasing boys."

Caroline responds with an icy stare. The line of her mouth is straight, but Louisa Nell detects a hidden sneer. Hateful girl. Pimple face. If you were my kid, thinks Louisa Nell, I'd choke you.

Caroline looks at Sandra to see if she's watching, then rolls her eyes again.

None of this is lost on Louisa Nell, who never had children but knows how to deal with them. She comes down off the stage and whispers in Caroline's ear, inhales the scent of her perfume, "Sweet Honesty" from Avon. "I don't want to worry you none," she says, "but with your eyes rolling around that way, I'd say you might be having an epileptic fit."

Sandra fusses. "It's not fair to have secrets," she pouts. "Y'all better let me in on it, too."

Delphine comes in from the kitchen carrying a pan of marshmallow crispies. Louisa Nell sighs and looks away. She was hoping for doughnuts. Delphine sets the refreshments on the coffee table, places a container of Handi-Wipes beside them, and slinks out onto the porch. "I'd give anything to be somebody," Delphine might as well say.

The trouble with Delphine is that she was born a Pruett. She's in awe of musical things. She's always felt inferior to the Fitzwaters, who can sing, every one of them, and have been able to since birth. "There's not a singing bone in my body," Delphine likes to lament, and her narrow shoulders droop when she says it, making her look like some gangly, melancholy bird. There is nothing sadder and more unattractive, thinks Louisa Nell, than a woman without hope.

But Delphine has hope for her daughters. She's grateful for what Louisa Nell is doing for her girls. "I just want 'em to be better'n me. I want 'em to have a chance," Delphine said two years ago when the singing sessions started. She clutched at her sister-in-law with her bony, dishwater-chapped hands, held on to her like she thought Louisa Nell had the keys to Nashville.

"Bless your heart," Louisa Nell said, putting an arm around Delphine, comforting her. "Course you do. And I'm gonna do what I can to help. There comes a time in a woman's life when she just wants to do something for others. I don't know. Maybe it's the religion coming out. You just get the feeling you want to pay back a little of all that's been given to you." Louisa Nell sighed. "Tell you what. I'm willing to help your girls all I can, but I'm counting on you to do your part."

Delphine shook her head and looked pitiful. "I don't know nothing about music."

"You don't have to," said Louisa Nell. "Leave the music to me. I'll teach 'em how to sing. It's your job to convince 'em that they want to."

Delphine got off easy the first year. Then Caroline started acting up. Louisa Nell has to hand it to her sister-in-law. She is a good disciplinarian. With a little coaxing, she can always be counted on to do what's right.

Louisa Nell fiddles with her tape recorder and clears her throat. "This afternoon we're gonna work on delivery," she says. I watched you girls at the county roundup. Your delivery stinks." It's true. They slur their words, frown when she tells them to smile. She practically has to thump them to get any vibrato in their voices. She stares at her nieces' youthful, unformed faces. If there's any determination there, she can't see it. Wastrels. They're going to blow it. She grabs one of Delphine's afghans from the back of the couch and dabs at the sweat on the back of her neck. Sometimes she wonders why she fools with the brats. She looks at Caroline. Lately, she's been slumping just for spite. "Stand up!" yells Louisa Nell when Caroline humps around like that. "Get those shoulders back." Last week, after the music session, Delphine came whispering around saying Caroline was self-conscious about her breasts. Louisa Nell told Delphine right in front of the girl that if she was her kid, she'd have her checked for scoliosis. Maybe fit her for a brace.

Outside, something that sounds like a lawn mower starts up. "Turn that thing off!" yells Louisa Nell, and she knocks over the autoharp leaning against the magazine rack as she strides toward the porch. She gives the magazine rack a swift kick and the May, June, and July issues of *Country Woman* slide onto the floor as though they've just been delivered.

"Kurt Weddle on his four-wheeler," says Sandra. "He's new. He moved here from Florida." She giggles and puts her hand over her mouth. "He was gonna give Caroline a ride."

Louisa Nell goes to the window and peeps through Delphine's venetian blinds. Kurt is looking toward the house. He revs the motor and sits there a minute as though waiting for something, then adjusts the chin strap on his helmet. When he puts the bike in gear, it jumps like an animal that's been shot. "Looks like he's changed his mind," says Louisa Nell as he drives away. She turns around and smiles at Caroline. Welcome to the world, girlie, she thinks. We've all got somewhere else we'd druther be.

Caroline lowers her cushion and leans forward on the couch as if she's about to charge. The veins in her neck stand out. Her face is so red she looks like she might be about to have a heatstroke.

Sandra digs at her ankles and shoots her sister a pleading glance. "Give you my lunch money for a week when school starts if you'll keep quiet," her look says. "Lunch money for a *whole* week."

Caroline stares at her sister a moment, then looks at Louisa Nell. "Wanta know what Kurt Weddle said about you?" she says. Her eyes glitter.

Louisa Nell folds her arms and looks away. "That boy doesn't even know me. I've never seen that boy in my life."

"Maybe not," says Caroline "but he's sure seen you. We were hiding in the corncrib when you drove up, and we peeked at you through the cracks." Caroline smiles. "We just stood out there and watched you lug your stuff into the house, and Kurt turns to me and says, 'Who the *hell* is that?' "

" 'And I say, 'Why, that there's my Aunt Louisa Nell, star of radio and stage.' "

" 'Could've fooled me,' says Kurt."

" 'And I say, 'My Aunt Louisa Nell's real good at that. She's fooled a lot of people. But she don't fool me about nothing. Not anymore.' "

For a moment, Louisa Nell doesn't move. Then slowly, as though she might need support, her hand floats out and comes to rest on the neck of the mike. The only sound in the room is the warning rattle of her bracelets. She shakes her head at Caroline as if to say, "You are either very stupid or too young to have figured certain things out."

Sandra begins to whimper.

Louisa Nell searches the house down for Delphine. This time she finds her out in the garden crawling around in the corn. The only clue to her whereabouts is the wiggling at the top of the dry yellow stalks.

Louisa Nell stands, feet planted wide in the sun-baked dirt. "Delphine, honey, what in the world you doing out here?"

"Checking the corn," says Delphine in a spider-web-thin voice.

Louisa Nell nods and looks up at the cloudless sky. "Nothing like a dry spell to ruin a good garden. If you ask me, I'd say you're more than a month too late." She smiles, flicks a potato beetle off her skirt. "Come on outa there," she says to Delphine. "If I didn't know better, I'd think you were hiding from me. You're needed in the house."

On the way, Delphine acts dizzy, disoriented, like she's been too long in the sun. Louisa Nell walks behind her and watches Delphine's callus-covered heels slide in and out of a pair of Buel's old shoes. Delphine stops beside the barn. On the other side, Buel is tapping on something. There is the flat sound of metal striking metal. He is less than a hundred feet away, but the echo wraps itself around and around the barn, making the distance seem much farther. Delphine leans against the rough, gray boards as though she is going to faint.

"They're good girls," she says, without turning around.

"Fine girls," says Louisa Nell. "And they've got you to thank."

Louisa Nell nudges Delphine toward the house. Delphine goes inside, puts her right hand over her heart as if she's about to say a pledge of allegiance, then backhands both her girls in the face. Delphine's mouth puckers as though she's the one who's been hit, and she runs and locks herself in the cellar. She won't come out.

"Come outa there!" says Louisa Nell. "Come outa there right this minute!"

But Delphine will not come out or answer no matter how hard Louisa Nell rattles the doorknob and says, "You only do it 'cause you love them. Deep down you know you're doing what's right."

After awhile, Louisa Nell gives up and goes back in the living room. She stops in the doorway and stares at her nieces' tear-streaked, angry faces. She is always fascinated by the handprint, red as a birthmark, across their smooth, young cheeks. She hasn't felt so alive since she was eleven and touched an electric fence.

Louisa Nell grips the mike, gives the center wheel a couple of turns and lowers the head to kid height. Suddenly, she is struck by an uncontrollable urge to snicker. She pretends to search for a pick in her purse. When she turns around, she stuffs half a marshmallow crispie into her mouth and chews. She presses her fingers together to check for stickiness, cleans them with a Handi-Wipe, then reaches for her guitar.

She clears her throat and steps up to the mike. "I'd like to start off with a little number that was voted song of the year back in 1976," she says, strumming, but somewhere inside her head, a tiny voice threatens to drown out the words to her song. She has no idea who the voice belongs to.

Louisa Nell looks at Sandra and winks, then glances at Caroline, who sits on the couch, clenching and unclenching her fists as though testing her strength. Sour note, thinks Louisa Nell. You'd ruin the tune of anybody's day.

Through the window, a yellow beam of sunlight cuts across the stage like a spotlight and stops a few inches short of Louisa Nell. It's late afternoon, but Nippy won't be home for his supper for another couple of hours. She cannot understand for the life of her why she feels pressed for time, cannot understand why she feels like another act is waiting just off-stage stamping its feet in the wings.

Testimony

Last night, at a revival in Carroll County, Brother Oren Hargle asked if we had loved ones in need of prayer. I sat there, wedged between a ferret-faced woman fanning herself with a hymnal on my left and an old man sleeping on my right, and let the Spirit move me. "I'd like you all to pray, if you would, for my sister Maureen," I said.

Brother Hargle squinted at me, the light in the church being bad, and it was clear he had no idea who I was or who Maureen was or why she needed prayer. How could he? I have attended the Grove Hill Baptist Church less than a week, have spent my summer going from revival to revival telling my story to all who have ears and will hear. It is the story of how a good girl can go bad and how a bad girl can go good, which just goes to show you the Lord really works in unpredictable ways.

"All right, sister," said Brother Hargle, a round little man whose bald head shines night and day as if reflecting heavenly light.

"Eunice," I said. "Call me Eunice."

"All right, Eunice," said Brother Hargle, scribbling in his prayer book. "What, exactly, is wrong with your sister?"

I stood, burdened by sin, before my brothers and sisters in Christ. "She's dead, Brother Hargle. Dead to the Lord and to her family, and I stand here tonight before God and all the rest of you to confess that I am at fault."

It was already 8:30 and almost time for "Dallas," but no one seemed in a hurry to leave. True, it's summer, and there's nothing on except reruns, but I'd like to think the frank and confidential nature of my confession also played a part. Who among us does not enjoy a good testimonial? The woman beside me ceased her fanning, the old man woke, jumping as if he'd been shot, and to my left, across the aisle, a mother unbuttoned her blouse and put her baby to her breast.

"Tell it, sister," sang Brother Hargle, and I did, same as it happened, same as I'd like to tell it to you. It's not a pretty story, but do not judge me hard; I am no longer the same woman I was back then. Confess your sins, and they will be forgiven, the Bible says. I live in Badden County, but the Bible doesn't say I have to confess over there. Wickedness finds more tolerance, I have discovered, the farther it gets from home.

If it's all right, I'd like to commence with a poem I wrote for Maureen, poetry writing being something I've done a lot of since I was Saved. There's not much else in Badden County for a Christian woman to do.

> Maureen, Maureen, born to blush unseen,
> Babe on your hip, thrice busted lip,

You led me to the Lord and you were lost,
And now my ransomed soul is tempest-tost.

A year ago, when it seemed likely Maureen would finish high school, Mama sent copies of her graduation picture and announcements to relatives as far away as Wilsonville, Nebraska, but it was great-uncle El, just down the road, who wrote back first and with the most enthusiasm. "You are a butiful girl," his letter said. "You got your great-grandmother's smile, your great-aunt Irma's eyes, and nothingthankGod from your father. Stay sweet. Hollywood will be calling."

"Doubtful," I said to myself at the time, given the fact that the telephone wires up to our house are buried in the creek bed in three places and flood season was upon us. Still, I sulked for days. Looking back on it, I was not a very nice person. I did not have Jesus in my life. If I was to meet my old self on the street today, I'd say, "Get thee behind me, Satan," and cross to the other side.

Maureen was my only sister, younger by four years. In our family there used to be a saying: "Maureen got the looks, and Eunice got the brains," which always seemed like a stingy way of looking at things, in my opinion, because it implied that Mama and Daddy didn't have enough of either to go around. But I was satisfied; "No Regrets" was my middle name. Durability is what counts in the long run, and thank God, I was blessed with qualities that last. There would've come a time in Maureen's life, say thirty, when her peachy cheeks would've paled, the skin on her neck sagged into wattles, and her blonde hair would've been seen for exactly what it was— an absence of color.

Maureen was thrilled by Uncle El's letter. Not because of his comments about her looks, which, in my honest opinion, were always quite ordinary, but because of his check for fifty dollars. When I graduated, bless his heart, he sent me twenty-five. Uncle El is my mother's mother's brother, a prostate-tormented old thing who ought to have been caught in the wheels of his own tractor years ago—according to Daddy. Uncle El used to work for a gas company, and he made some good investments. He never married or had any kids to spend his money on, which was the only reason we sent him announcements in the first place.

Daddy and Uncle El got in an argument about a borrowed ladder years ago and haven't been able to stand each other since. I am the spitting image of Daddy. One does not have to be a rocket scientist to figure certain things out.

Mama must've told Maureen I was upset about the money because in no time, Maureen was tap-tap-tapping at my bedroom door. One thing you need to know about Maureen: she was good in those days. What she lacked in common sense, she made up by being extra nice. She rescued wasps from spiders' webs, knowing full well that if given half a chance they'd sting her, cried over obituaries of people she didn't know, prayed for those no one else liked. "A little wickedness would make you a whole lot more interesting," I tried to tell her, but, wisely, she ignored the advice. Maureen was Saved when she was in the sixth grade, baptized in the swimming hole up the creek. After that, she and Mama hounded Daddy and me about taking the plunge. Our hearts were hard. We resisted.

Into my room came Maureen as if she'd been invited. She sat on my bed, folded her hands in her lap, and watched as I tried on a new teal eyeliner. "So," I go. "What brings our favorite niece to the working-class section of the house?"

"Oh, Eunie," she said. "I feel just awful about the money."

"I can tell," I said. "I'd feel the same if I was you." I sat at my dresser and looked at both our faces in the mirror. Maureen never wore make-up. If she had, she could have perked up her complexion and drawn attention away from a decidedly weak chin. "Born-agains have a certain glow," Mama used to tell me. "The world knows, just from looking at us, that we've been changed from the inside out." I compared the skin tones in our faces, and one of us glowed, no doubt about it, but it was my skin instead of Maureen's, compliments of Merle Norman's Heavenly Rose Creamy Blusher.

Maureen picked at the lint balls on my bedspread. I could tell that something charitable was up. "What's half of twenty-five?" she asked. This from a senior in high school. Not to be ugly or anything, but Maureen bypassed the really tough courses. Instead, she filled her schedule with Typing I and II, Driver's Ed, Beginning Sewing, and Marriage & the Family. You couldn't load up on fluff like that when I was in school. It's shocking the changes that can occur in such a short time. A few weeks back, I attended a donkey ball game at the high school, and instead of watching the game, I just sat on the bleachers, looked around the dingy gym, and cried. Makes me sick to see how the place has gone downhill.

"What do you think I am, a walking calculator?" I said to her. Dividing twenty-five by two isn't all that hard, I know, but Maureen graduated with a 2.0 average. I, on the other hand, took every math course Farlanburg High offered, and my grade point average, as you may have guessed, was still a full point higher. During my four years of math, I also learned from watching my teachers that the surest way to seem smart and hoodwink others is to make a task seem harder than it really is. "This'll take a minute," I told her. "What you got in mind?"

I was not surprised by Maureen's next gesture. "Uncle El gave you twenty-five; he gave me fifty. That really isn't fair," she said in what I used to call her best I-took-Jesus-as-my-savior-you-take-him-too voice. "We'll just take the extra twenty-five he gave me and divide it in half. That'd make it even. Right?"

I closed my eyes and pretended to calculate. After a minute, I opened one eye and shook my head.

Maureen frowned, disappointment clouding her normally sunny face.

"There's nothing wrong with your figuring," I told her, "but I can't accept your gift. If Uncle El had wanted me to have the money, he would've given it to me. Obviously, he thought your future was a wiser investment."

Maureen looked stricken. The quickest way to cause one of the Flock to blow a logic fuse, I had learned, was to overload his circuits with guilt. Force him to carry that guilt until his conscience sent little messages down his spine—plinga, plinga, plinga—prompting his arms to dump whatever you wanted right in your lap. In this case, prolonging Maureen's guilt had the effect of upping the size of the kitty. "Oh, Eunie," she said, eyes bright with tears, "I can't believe Uncle El could be so unfair."

I shook my head, sadly. "Not unfair, really. Insensitive is more like it."

Maureen wiped her eyes. "Here. I want you to have it. All of it." She got up from the bed, pulled the money from her skirt pocket, and before I could say, "Praise the Lord," she hugged me and forfeited the entire fifty. I protested just enough to seem Christian, wretch that I was, then gave in, remarking that her generosity seemed to make her truly happy.

"Oh it does! It does!" exclaimed Maureen, and given her tendency toward honesty, I couldn't bring myself to doubt her.

Afterwards, she must have worried she'd been too hard on Uncle El because she stopped on her way out the door and turned just as I was admiring the crispness of the bills. "In my heart of hearts, I know Uncle El didn't mean to hurt your feelings," she said. "He's just getting old, and his memory is short."

I nodded, but in my heart of hearts, I knew I was young and mine was long.

Taking advantage of the innocent and feeble-minded is not something I'm particularly proud of. I confess it to you with sorrow in my heart. But it was Maureen's innocence that got her into trouble in the first place. She went behind Daddy's back and broke one of his policies, and I don't see how I'm to blame for that.

Daddy has policies: about education, dating, and life. "I have this policy," Daddy is always saying, and I admire him so much, I have adopted some of them myself. His policies for Maureen and me were good ones, designed for our own protection and simple enough for even Maureen to understand. "Young folks are full of foolishness and need guidelines," says Daddy. I couldn't agree with him more.

Daddy's Education Policy: NO QUITTING BEFORE YOU ARE SIXTEEN. GRADUATE AND I'LL BUY YOU A CAR. Daddy quit when he was in fifth grade, and he says it was the biggest mistake of his life. Daddy lays pipeline, works all over the state during the spring, summer, and fall. Pipeliners make big money. When I graduated, he bought me a Mustang—one owner, tilt steering wheel, cruise control.

Daddy's Dating Policy: NO BEARDS, NO CATHOLICS, NO HONKERS
TOO LAZY TO COME TO THE DOOR. "I'll kill the man who ever takes
advantage of you girls," Daddy used to say, and he clenched
his fists and made ripping noises with his mouth to prove it.

"He just doesn't want you to get mixed up with riffraff,"
Mama explained. I could see her point.

Daddy and Mama never have to worry about me in that
department. I never give them a minute's trouble. The night
of my senior prom, I helped Mama plant potatoes. "I'd think
you'd miss being out with people your own age," said Mama.
"Dancing with all those nice boys."

I dropped enough seed potatoes in the ground to finish out
the row, then picked up a rock and smashed dirt clods. "I'd
rather garden any ole day than waste my time at a dance," I
told her. "I have *nothing* in common with any of the boys in
my class."

The day after graduation, I went to work as an assistant to
the Badden County Assessor. I have an office in the courthouse. We go around to people's homes and ask them how
many cars, dogs, and acres they own. That way, we know
how much to tax them. I post myself at the back door while he
knocks at the front. You'd be surprised how many people try
to sneak out.

"The courthouse is a good place to meet people," said
Mama. "I have a feeling you'll meet lots of boys you have
something in common with over there."

So far, I haven't.

Maureen dated a lot in high school, but that was because
Mama set her up with boys from our church. "Good boys,"
said Mama, "from Christian families." On her dates, Maureen
went to church potlucks and funerals and sing-alongs. I never
cared for such activities myself.

As far back as I can remember, Mama had to keep an eye on Maureen. "Your sister's not like you," Mama once told me, which was unnecessary because I'd already figured that out. "Maureen is special, Eunice, honey. She's . . . what's the word for it?"

"Retarded," I snickered.

"Stop being ugly!" said Mama. She thought a moment. "What I'm trying to say is that Maureen is naive. To her, the world smells like a honeysuckle garden. That's admirable, but not very practical. One thing we all have to learn, sooner or later, is that the world stinks. If it didn't, what would be the point of Heaven?" Mama sighed. "Your sister has been blessed with this beautiful face. Surely you've noticed. And she has a heart as good as—"

"Gold," I said, sourly.

"That's right," said Mama, putting her arm around me and giving my shoulder a little squeeze. "The combination of those two things can get her in a lot of trouble. There are ornery people in the world, Eunice, who won't think twice about taking advantage of your sister. We need to look out for her. Do you understand?"

"You can count on me, Mama," I replied.

Mama's outlook on life may sound a trifle pessimistic, especially for a Christian. There are two types of Believers, I have observed: those who *know* God is going to destroy the world again but really see no need for it, and those who *know* it's going to happen and think tomorrow isn't soon enough. Being the cheerful sort, I tend toward the former; Mama, like most of our congregation, does not. "Doom and gloom," groans Daddy. This is one aspect of religion that turns him off.

Maureen never had sense enough to know she was supposed to have an opinion. God could've wiped out the world, with her in it, and that would've been fine with Maureen. To her, being a Believer meant saying NO to drugs and not hurting people or animals. I doubt she ever gave important religious issues a moment's thought.

During the spring of her senior year, unbeknownst to Mama or Daddy, she took up with a boy named Reggie Tuggle, one of five Tuggle brothers who live with their father on the Clendenin side of the Little Pine River. There's Ronnie, Reggie, Richie, Raymond, and Roger—the Tuggle brothers. There used to be one named Randall, who was between Reggie and Richie. He drowned.

Maureen wasn't the sort to go against one of Daddy's policies, but she had a weak spot in her heart for hoods and outcasts. Don't we all. "Jesus loves them same as He loves us," she always said whenever the subject of hoods and outcasts came up. "They're such nice people when you really get to know them."

"Trust me," said Daddy. "They'll outgrow it."

The Tuggles live in a house with no floor. I've heard they tore it up, board by board, for firewood. The Tuggles are crazy, people say, and as far as I'm concerned, that proves it. They're a scruffy bunch: slope-shouldered, bushy-browed, and motherless. Rumor has it that when the sixth one, Roger, was born, Belva Tuggle took one look at him, saw that he matched the others, then threw up her hands and left. Some say she remarried and found a better life in Ohio. Daddy swears he saw her, two years ago, standing on a street corner in Charleston. Uncle El says she never left town at all, that she's holed up at the Jarrett's Hotel, Norm Jarrett's private plaything. "Wherever she is," says Mama, "she left her kids, and you can be sure she'll rot in Hell."

I went to school with Richie, the middle Tuggle. The only

thing I remember about him is something that happened in fifth grade. I tell it only to give a clear picture of what the Tuggles are really like. It was winter, the middle of February, and Richie had a sore throat. The principal said it was probably strep, and he told Richie not to come back to school till he went to a doctor. Richie's daddy took him to Doc Harkins in town, and Doc gave him a little bottle of pink medicine. "Keep refrigerated. Shake well," the instructions said. The Tuggles didn't have a refrigerator, but it was plenty cold outside, so Richie's daddy locked him in a shed overnight and gave him a good shaking the next morning before he brought him in. That's what Richie told when he came back to school.

"You are such a liar," said Jennifer Barnett, one of the town kids in our class.

Mrs. O'Dell, our teacher, agreed. "There are better ways to get attention, Richie," she said. "Try doing something constructive with your life." She handed him the *Weekly Reader* he'd missed, and because he still looked contagious, she pointed to a chair in the back of the room.

When I went to get my coat for recess, I dropped a note on Richie's desk. "I believe you," the note said, and when he read it, he grinned, rubbed the mole on the back of his crusty neck, and adored me the rest of the year. Just goes to show you a Tuggle doesn't even know when it's been insulted.

"The poor always ye have with you," the Good Book says, and I know, for a fact, that it's true. Ever since I can remember, a Tuggle has been rowing itself across the river so it can catch the bus and go to school. The mud bank in front of their house is slick with their comings and goings. They usually attend until the seventh or eighth grade, then they stop. A Tuggle just doesn't have what it takes to go any further.

Reggie is no exception, though he is the smartest and best-looking one in his family. He quit his freshman year in high school. Someone said he was a drug addict for a while, but I doubt it. From what I have heard, being a drug addict takes money, which a Tuggle does not have. I have never known a Tuggle to work. I don't know what Reggie was doing hanging around the parking lot at the high school, but that's where Maureen met him. I am as romantic as the next person, but it's hard to imagine love blossoming between the buses. "Get a job! Develop a work ethic!" I would have said to him if he'd tried to put the moves on me.

Maureen began going out with Reggie Tuggle. I might never have known a thing about it if she hadn't confessed. We were taking turns mowing the yard one evening. It was late March, I remember, because Mama yelled out the window and told us not to mow over her Star of Bethlehem flowers under the tree in the front yard. I had just finished my ten laps around the house with the lawn mower and had passed it to Maureen. The mower smelled hot, and Maureen bent over to dislodge a grass ball that was clogging the blower hole. As she did, a ring, attached to a chain around her neck, spilled from the front of her blouse. The ring was silver, man-sized, with a black stone. *Cheap* is what I thought. "If I am not mistaken, you are wearing a new piece of jewelry," I shouted above the noise of the motor. "It's not mine, and it's not Mama's. Did you get it from a boy?"

Maureen took off with the mower and did a couple of laps. Another thing about Maureen: she could be stubborn. I sat on the front porch steps and waited for her to come back around the house, then gave her my traffic light routine. "Red light!" I said, jumping directly in her path.

She screamed and jerked the mower to the right, which caused Mama to lose six out of nine surviving tulips planted next to the front steps. "That was stupid!" she yelled, her face turning red. "I could have cut off your feet!"

I looked at the pink and yellow tulips scattered like confetti around the yard. "Correct," I replied, "and all because you were selfish and wouldn't share your secret."

Maureen fiddled with the throttle lever and refused to look at me.

"Fess up," I said. "You're wasting gas."

She folded her arms and stared into the woods behind our house. Finally, she shut off the mower. "Can I trust you?" she asked.

With that, I nudged her out of the way, put my foot on the side of the mower, and gave the starter a good yank.

"What's the matter?"

"What do you think's the matter?" I said. "If you don't know by now whether you can trust me, there's nothing I can say or do to make you decide."

"Oh, Eunie," she said. "I didn't mean it like that."

"The hell you didn't," I told her. I cussed a lot in those days, I must confide.

She hugged me and I let her, and I could tell there was something she needed to get off her chest. So I took her by the hand, and we went into the woods and sat down on the moss bed where we played when we were little. "Start at the beginning," I said, "and don't leave anything out."

Maureen was nervous. She began to pull little plugs of moss from the bed, and she'd plucked a circle at least six inches in diameter before she finally began to talk. "Do you ever wonder why you were put here on earth?" she asked.

"No," I said. "Quit stalling."

Maureen fingered the chain around her neck. "I think God has a plan for each of us. A job he sent us here to do."

I pictured myself wandering the halls of the court house, winning souls in the magistrate's office, holding the record for the highest number of conversions in the Xerox room. "The *ring,*" I said, pointing to Maureen's chest. "Tell me about the *ring.*"

Maureen leaned toward me. "If I do, you've got to promise you won't tell Mama or Daddy. They won't understand."

I put my hand on her shoulder. "Trust me."

She pulled the ring from her shirt. "It belongs to Reggie Tuggle," she said.

At first, I was unable to move. They say that happens when a body is in shock. I sat there, legs crossed Indian-style, and listened. For three months, Maureen had been meeting Reggie Tuggle on her lunch hour. While her friends were in the cafeteria making fun of the teachers and tossing hamburger Frisbees, Maureen was on a mission in the parking lot.

"God has allowed me to be an instrument of change," she said, "and he is working through me to improve Reggie's life. Since I've been seeing Reggie, he hasn't had a drop to drink. He's given up smoking, has quit stealing, and he doesn't even cuss. He wants to marry me."

"How do you know?" I asked.

Maureen looked confused. "Because he asked me. Face to face."

"I *assumed* that," I said. "How do you know he's quit drinking and stealing?"

"He told me," she said.

Forgive me if I seem skeptical concerning the forthrightness of a fellow human being, but this was a Tuggle we were discussing, which is ample reason to doubt. "What about a job? Has he got a job?"

"He will have," said Maureen. "In time."

I looked at her.

"God is using me," she said, happily.

He's not the only one, I thought.

Maureen picked at the moss again. "I'll tell you something else if you promise not to tell."

"You're pregnant," I said. "You've done it with Reggie Tuggle, and you're going to have his baby."

Maureen frowned and shook her head.

I reconsidered. "You've done it with more than one of the Tuggles, and you don't know which one is the father."

Maureen blushed. "I'm teaching Reggie how to read," she said, proudly.

This was not at all what I'd expected, and I must admit to a feeling akin to disappointment. There is a dark side to all of us when Satan rules our hearts. I stared at the house and listened to the wind, a pale green whisper in the trees.

"You don't approve," said Maureen. "I can tell."

"I didn't say that," I told her. "It's just that, being your sister, I want what's best for you. Can I help it if I have questions?"

"Like what?" she asked.

"If you marry him, where will you live? How will you eat?"

"I'll stay here at home until I graduate," said Maureen.

"Not if Daddy finds out."

"He won't. By the time he does, he'll have changed his mind about Reggie. I have faith that it will all work out."

I laughed.

"What's the matter?" said Maureen.

"Nothing," I told her. "But I must say you surprise me. Sneaking around behind Daddy's back, breaking one of his policies. If I didn't know you'd been Saved, I'd swear you were as wicked as me."

Maureen grabbed my hand; she was a toucher. "Oh,
Eunie," she said. "Don't talk that way. You're not wicked.
Just because you haven't been Saved doesn't mean you're
bad. No one can see into another person's heart."

"True," I agreed, but I tell you, brothers and sisters, the
world would be a better place, and Maureen's fate might have
been different, if we were forced to wear our hearts on our
sleeves and those hearts were as transparent as glass.

We sat there in silence, Maureen playing with the ring and
chain and me watching ants lug white things in and out of a
hole where Maureen had pulled up the moss.

"What would you do if it was you?" she said. "Would you
marry him?"

I looked at my sister, so innocent, so trusting, and saw my
reflection in her eyes. If I'd looked long enough, I'd have seen
the devil sitting there beside me. "The world is full of
choices," I heard Daddy saying. "As you walk along the Great
Highway of Life, you will come to many forks in the road,
where you will have to decide whether to go left or right."
Daddy has always been somewhat of a philosopher.

"What do you think?" said Maureen.

I glanced at her, then quickly looked away. If I was a ser-
pent, then she was a bare heel begging to be bit.

"Say something," she said.

So I did. "Maureen, honey, I want you to know I admire
your generosity of spirit and applaud your Christian attitude.
A Tuggle might not be my choice for a husband, but who am I
to argue? Success tells its own tale. If you have accomplished
so much with Reggie on your lunch hour, I marvel to think
what could happen if you had him round-the-clock."

One week later, on a Friday afternoon,
Maureen ran off with Reggie Tuggle. The woods were lacy

with new leaves, the air sweet and delicately perfumed. I cannot envision a more perfect season for love. From what I have been able to piece together, they met in the parking lot at school, hitchhiked to Clendenin, and enlisted the services of a Rev. Willard B. Worley.

Daddy came home from pipelining on Friday evening, bone-tired but richer. I had baked a hummingbird cake for him, his favorite. He was halfway through his second piece when he looked at me and said, "Where's Maureen?"

"Am I my sister's keeper?" I asked.

"Don't be a smark aleck," said Daddy, which hurt me to no end.

"She didn't get off the bus this evening," said Mama. "Something must've come up, and she had to stay late at school. If she calls while I'm out in the garden, holler, and I'll go get her."

I did the dishes and was not surprised when seven o'clock rolled around and there was still no sign of Maureen. Mama and Daddy were worried. Mama called a couple of Maureen's friends, but they hadn't seen her. I didn't know where she was for sure, but I had my suspicions.

At 7:30, Daddy decided to go into town to look for her. First, he wanted to call the sheriff's office. Mama followed him into the living room and sat on the couch while he dialed. "This is so embarrassing," she said. "What are people gonna think if a police car passes up the road and pulls in at our house?"

I have never been one to take pleasure in the discomfort of others. Worry, I have read, can cause all sorts of health-related problems. "Stop!" I said.

Daddy put his hand over the receiver and looked at me.

"What is it?" said Mama.

I put my fingers to my temples and shut my eyes. "I don't

know, exactly," I told them, "but I feel sort of funny."

"Go feel funny somewhere else," said Daddy, but when I swooned and fell between the couch and the recliner, he hung up and rushed to my side.

"Don't move," said Mama. She grabbed a cushion and propped it under my head. "Just stay put and tell me where it hurts."

"It doesn't hurt anywhere, Mama," I told her. "It's the most peaceful feeling I've ever had in my life."

She brought me a cold washcloth and arranged it on my forehead. "You're probably anemic," she said. "My mother was anemic once, and it did her the same way."

I lay there, relishing her ministering. There is nothing so comforting as a mother's hand on the brow. She and Daddy seemed relieved when I sat up and removed the washcloth. "I know this is going to sound silly," I said, "but I think I've just discovered where Maureen is."

"She's delirious," Mama said out of the corner of her mouth.

"No I'm not," I assured her. I looked at Daddy. "I don't know quite how to tell you this, but I think I've had a religious experience." I lowered my voice and shut my eyes. "I cannot say for sure, but I suspect it was a vision."

"You're right," said Daddy. "It sounds silly." I understood his reaction: He felt betrayed. All those years, he and I had held out together, perennial heathens outnumbered ten to one. We gave each other strength.

"Hush! Let her talk," said Mama, taking hold of my arm.

This brings me to the most loathsome part of my story. But let he who has not stretched the truth to save his own hide at some point be the first one to cast a stone. Is self-preservation not among the strongest of instincts? Will a drowning man not lap his legs around his brother or stand on his own mother's head for a breath of air?

"A glass of water would be nice," I said, and Mama ran to get it. I watched her all the way to the kitchen; it was easier than looking at Daddy. "I'm not sure how to explain any of this," I said when she returned, "but I had this picture in my head. I saw a *huge* mountain ringed by seven suns. Around each of the seven suns were seven stars and around the seven stars were seven lamps, each pouring oil toward the foot of the mountain. At the bottom of the mountain stood two sheep, one playing a saxophone and one playing a trombone. On the saxophone were six eagles, and on the trombone were six lions, each with a gold ring around its neck."

"Go on," said Mama.

"That's it," I replied.

Mama turned to Daddy and frowned. "It sounds exactly like something out of the book of Revelation," she said. "What on earth do you think—?"

"Excuse me," I interrupted. "I know I haven't had much experience with visions, but I have the strangest feeling it means that Maureen ran off and got married."

Daddy scowled. "What the hell are you talking about?" Like so many of those who are unSaved, Daddy is prone to cuss, particularly when he is under stress. He grabbed me by my arm, pulled me to my feet, then shook me as if he thought truth can be got from a sinner as easily as apples from a tree.

"According-to my-interp-retation-she's gone-and married-one of-Axel-Tuggle's-boys," I managed to say between shakes.

Daddy stopped and looked at me. "That's the silliest vision

I ever heard," he said. "Try harder." He shook me again and said it didn't take a church-going man to recognize blasphemy. About that time, Maureen walked in.

"Where have you been?" demanded Daddy.

Maureen put her books and her purse on the coffee table, then looked at me. "At school," she said, which was probably the first lie she'd ever told in her life, God bless her.

"Your sister," said Daddy, glaring at me, "has been ranting about you and one of Axel Tuggle's boys. Says she had a vision that meant you'd gone and gotten married."

Maureen swallowed, and her face turned white.

"It's not true is it?" said Daddy, and when Maureen didn't say anything, Mama cupped her hands over her mouth.

"Say something!" said Daddy, and when Maureen finally did, Mama wilted, and Daddy had to help her to the couch. I found the washcloth and handed it to Daddy, then glanced at Maureen, who was looking at me like she was seeing me for the first time in her life.

"You could always have it annulled," I said to her, which seemed the practical solution.

"If you knew the Word like you ought to," wailed Mama, "you'd know that man cannot undo what God has done."

"God had nothing to do with the business that has taken place tonight," said Daddy. "This is the work of the devil himself."

Maureen started to say something, then, without warning, began to cry. Next thing we knew, she turned, threw open the screen door, and ran out of the house. Daddy was right behind her; Mama followed. I pulled back the curtain and watched out the living room window, which gave me a clear view. It was almost dark. Daddy stopped on the front porch, his skin yellow under the bug light. He shouted at Maureen, who was running through the yard. "Come back here!" yelled Daddy, but Maureen just kept on going.

"Do something!" said Mama, giving him a little shove.

Daddy ran down the steps and out the walk, his house shoes flapping on his heels. "If you take another step, girl," he said, "you'll be making the biggest mistake of your life. You hear me?"

Maureen was more than halfway down the driveway, whizzing out and away from us like a comet.

"If you leave this yard," roared Daddy, "it's gonna be damned near impossible for you to come back! Count on it. You spend one night with a Tuggle, you'll be dead as far as I'm concerned! Good-bye Daddy, good-bye Mama, good-bye cushy life!"

Maureen turned left near the mailbox and began to hotfoot it down the dirt road that would take her to the mouth of the hollow.

"Maureen!" screamed Mama. "I'm going after her," she said to Daddy, but Daddy is strong from lifting pipelines, and he blocked her with his arm.

"You're going nowhere," he informed her. "Give her half an hour. Ten dollars says she'll turn back before she crosses the Sutliff Bridge."

Some people are stubborn. Daddy is one of them. He has this policy: A MAN IS ONLY AS GOOD AS HIS WORD. A MAN'S WORD IS HIS BOND. "I say what I mean, and I mean what I say," says Daddy, which, in Maureen's case, when she didn't return, meant good-bye. I suppose we all have our shortcomings.

For three weeks, Mama set a plate for Maureen at the table. Old habits die hard. Maureen moved in with the Tug-

gles, we heard. Reliable sources confirmed it. Carol Ann Bes-
hear, who works at the county clerk's office, said she was
driving down the highway a couple of days later, happened to
look across the river, and saw a girl who looked a lot like
Maureen being wallowed by several Tuggles in the front
yard. Mama went into hysterics when she heard it. She
begged Daddy to let her go get Maureen, to let her tell Maureen all was forgiven and she could come home, but Daddy
stood his ground.

"She made her bed. Let her lie in it," said Daddy. It is
typical of the unSaved to be so hard, I have found.

"I don't think the Tuggles have beds," I said, thinking a
little humor might help.

"Keep it up," said Daddy, "and there'll be two birds missing from the nest."

Uncle El took the news pretty hard. I delivered it the day
after Maureen left, along with a pan of apple crisp I had baked.
I wanted Uncle El to hear it from me before he heard it from
someone else. That's what family is for. He sat on his back
porch and cried when I told him, then he took his cane and
whacked one of his cats. He kept confusing Maureen with his
dead sister, Irma. "She was a *butiful* girl," he said, wiping
tears from his eyes. In addition to having a faulty prostate, his
mind is also going.

Maureen, I am sorry to report, did not graduate. When the
list of seniors and commencement pictures appeared in the
county paper, neither her name nor her likeness was among
them. Mama called the school to find out what had happened,
and the principal informed her Maureen hadn't set foot on the
school grounds for the last seven weeks of the term, which
gave her zeros on all her finals—a snafu, he said, there was
just no getting round.

Nor has she set foot in our church for almost a year now. She could have switched to a different denomination, but that's doubtful, given the kind of language I recently heard her use. A few weeks ago, on a Saturday, Mama sent me to buy tomato plants. "Get the Beefsteaks and not the Early Birds," she said, and I just about wore myself out running all over town. I had come out of the hardware store and had taken a shortcut to the parking lot through an alley. Garbage cans and empty boxes lined both sides of the narrow street, and the air conditioners lifted my skirt with little gusts of hot wind. I was hurrying along, my arms full of tomato flats, when who should I stumble onto but Maureen. She was sitting on the steps behind Meacham's Restaurant, quite pregnant, and eating French burnt peanuts out of a sack. In front of her sat a rusty red wagon containing two scantly filled grocery bags. She had put on an unflattering amount of weight, particularly on her upper arms and thighs, and I was almost on top of her before I recognized who it was. "Maureen!" I shouted, unable to curb my joy and surprise.

Maureen turned her head and looked at me, and I must say I was astonished that a single year could effect such a change. Her left eye was black and swollen, while the right one was still in a green stage of recuperation. Her nose, which had always been perky and somewhat turned up at the end, was much flatter and had been artlessly repositioned to one side. It was hard to tell from her expression whether she was in the mood for questions. "Sister," I said, gently, "it appears you have been involved in a little scrape."

Maureen chewed her peanuts and looked at me, then slowly raised her hand and swatted at a fly. She leaned forward and seemed to be searching for something in her grocery bag, and I assumed we were about to have a sister-to-sister talk over a picnic lunch. I bent over to put my plants down, wondering whether I ought to suggest a more pleasant location, and it was then she walloped me with a tin can in the side of the head and let loose a string of obscenities, the specifics of which I will not go into, because it would take too long and besides, the words are too vile.

Judging by the depth of the wound, it was a big can—at least 28 ounces. The blow caught me just behind my right ear, and for a brief moment, I couldn't tell sky from alley. Next thing I remember, I was making a run for the parking lot, followed closely by Maureen, who continued to curse and pelt me with round after round of potatoes, canned vegetables, and potted meat.

To make a long story short, I escaped without serious bodily harm. I considered pressing charges but decided against it because I have never been one to seek revenge. Nor did I report the incident at home. Daddy does not want Maureen's name mentioned in our house, and I do not want either Mama or Daddy to know what a base person their daughter has become. The true test of a Believer's faith, I have always said, is not how he handles himself during the good times, but how well he copes during the bad. Job, with all his trials and afflictions, never made such a fuss or behaved as badly as Maureen.

She has a baby now, though none of us has seen it. Like the rest of the Tuggles, it's probably slope-shouldered, bushy-browed, and unchurched. Whatever it is, is immaterial to us, says Daddy, because *our* Maureen died.

So. How do I live with myself, you wonder? Coping with even small amounts of guilt is always hard. If it hadn't been for the support of my church family, which I joined soon after Maureen left us, I cannot say where my misery might have led me. Friends, I do not have to tell you the difference a trip to the creek can make in your life. When I took the plunge less than a year ago, I emerged a changed woman, at peace with myself, new in Christ. "Do you mean to tell me this one act can wipe out every hateful thing I've ever done?" I asked our pastor as he led me into the water.

"It can if you believe it can," he replied.

"But I've been so full of orneriness," I told him. "I've done some wicked things in my life."

" 'Ask, and it shall be given you;' " he said, " 'seek, and ye shall find; knock, and it shall be opened unto you.' "

"Amazing," I said, even as he dunked me. Afterwards, I was surprised that no neighbors downstream reported that their water had run black.

I emerged forgiven, with a certificate to prove it. Being human, I constantly have to guard against doubt, particularly late at night when I am alone in my room, and it hops and plays in a corner of my mind like a mouse.

"What does the Bible tell you about repentance?" Brother Hargle said after I had finished my testimony last night.

"It's on the tip of my tongue," I said. "Give me a clue."

"There is more joy in Heaven over one sinner who repents than over ninety nine respectable people who do not need to repent!" he thundered, and with that, the entire congregation shouted, "Amen!" and rushed to hug me.

To date, I have spoken in all adjacent counties, twenty-seven different churches, to be exact. I asked and I received; I sought, and I did find. I knocked and all kinds of doors have opened unto me. I have taken a pledge to spread the good news to others, to go forth filled with confidence and conviction, a steadfast soldier of Christ.

"Spread it wherever you want," says Daddy, "but I better

never hear of you telling family secrets or airing our dirty laundry in this county."

If you say a prayer for Maureen, please throw one in for Daddy, won't you?

The Retirement Party

I t is two o'clock on a Friday afternoon
in April. The willows along the river north of town are a
tender grasshopper green; patches of henbit and bitter cress
sprout like tufts of hair in the winter-weary yards. In the
basement of the library on Main Street, Miss Lucy McKewn,
age thirty-six, assistant librarian, cleans up the last of the
cookie crumbs left by the Story Hour children. She is a local
woman, Farlanburg born, a member of that category often
referred to as "attractive enough"—though no one ever says
attractive enough for what. She wears her straight brown hair
pulled back from her face by barrettes, which, at a distance,
look like hyphens above her ears. Using the side of her hand,
she rakes cookie scraps into piles, eats the chunks, then
sweeps the rest off the table and into the garbage can.

When she finishes cleaning, she goes upstairs to Microfilm

and debates whether she ought to call Jack at the deli to
remind him about Mrs. Worsham's party, which is scheduled
for four o'clock this afternoon. She doesn't look forward to
the party, but she'd rather be there than at home, a three-
room apartment above the garage of a Mr. and Mrs. W. T.
Tucker on Stringer Street. Come September, Miss Lucy will
have lived in her garage apartment fourteen years—a fact
that might not depress her if she could forget that she origi-
nally told the Tuckers she'd be staying only two.

The cookie crumbs have roused her hunger. Her stomach
roils and growls. As she rewinds film onto the proper spools,
a task the Historical Society ladies are forever forgetting to
do, the machine creaks and sings to her and seems to say,
"Lemon Cremes or Lorna Doones? Lemon Cremes or Lorna
Doones?"

At the front desk, Mrs. Worsham, the librarian, prunes her
spider plant and talks to Shirley, who teaches Adult Ed. Shirley skims a newspaper. She has assigned her students a difficult math problem. They sit at a table back in Fiction, rubbing their foreheads and chewing on their pencils. Today,
Mrs. Worsham and Shirley are having a discussion about "the
good life" and the fact that more people have it in small towns
than in large ones. Miss Lucy leans against the microfilm
machine and listens. "Your small towns are where you find
your happy people," says Mrs. Worsham. "In your small
towns, you've got your close families, your safe streets, and
your clean air."

Shirley smiles as though she has a secret. She says she
wonders. She says she's not so sure. Unlike Mrs. Worsham
and Miss Lucy, Shirley hasn't lived her whole life in a small
town. The only reason she is in this one is because she met
and married Russ Keller, a local boy.

"Well I'm sure," says Mrs. Worsham. She snips and coifs

married Russ," Mrs. Worsham says to Shirley. She gives her plant a drink.

Shirley moistens her finger with her tongue and turns a page of the newspaper. She does not always feel compelled to speak when spoken to. Mrs. Worsham says that's because Shirley was raised in New Jersey where good manners are a thing of the past. "You can't expect her to change overnight," Mrs. Worsham tells the Historical Society ladies when they complain that Shirley is rude.

Shirley met Russ several years ago while he was in the Army and stationed at Fort Dix. For the first few years of their marriage, they lived in New Jersey, but last year, Russ brought Shirley home to Farlanburg. Since then, he has worked for his father, who owns a rock quarry on the outskirts of town. Russ is an only child, and one day, if he behaves himself, he will own a ton of rock. Several hundred tons, in fact. Rumor has it that Shirley says owning a rock quarry is about as exciting as owning the county dump. Just last week, Mrs. Worsham told Miss Lucy she heard that Shirley is leaving; despite nine years of marriage and two kids, Shirley is calling it quits. "I don't know what's the matter with people these days that they can't just settle down and be happy. I'm happy," said Mrs. Worsham. "Thirty years I've worked at one job. Been married to the same man for thirty-seven." Mrs. Worsham shook her head. "Elba Mounts said she heard Shirley is taking the two little boys and going back to New Jersey as soon as school is out. I can't believe Shirley wouldn't say anything to us. You know anything about it?"

"No," said Miss Lucy, but she was sad to hear it. Shirley has worked at the library less than six months. She has triple-pierced ears, short, dark hair, and she's the only woman Miss Lucy knows who has given herself permission to cuss. She seems much younger than thirty-five. Shirley keeps to herself a lot, so Miss Lucy doesn't really know her. "Surly Shirley," Mrs. Worsham calls her. But her presence in Farlanburg gives Miss Lucy something she cannot explain. Coming to the library each morning and seeing Shirley makes Miss Lucy feel the same way she does when she walks into the grocery store and sees a kiwi fruit or a coconut in June.

Mrs. Worsham takes a bottle of Miracle-Gro from her desk and squeezes two green drops onto the soil around her plant. "Personally, I think there's no place like a small town to raise kids."

Shirley shrugs and says she wouldn't know.

"The good thing about a town this size is that it's safe. You can just turn the little devils loose and let them run."

Shirley says that may be, but her boys prefer organized sports and judo.

"Your boys remind me a lot of my boys when they were little," says Mrs. Worsham. "Just think. If you hadn't married Russ, you wouldn't have them. Close your eyes and try to imagine what your life would be like." Mrs. Worsham looks at Miss Lucy, then closes her eyes and tries to imagine. By the distressed look on her face, she clearly can't.

"Everything works out for the best in the long run," says Mrs. Worsham. "Just ask Miss Lucy. If she'd got it into her head to go chasing off somewhere right after she graduated from Farlanburg State, she'd never have the satisfaction of knowing she stayed and took care of her daddy during his old age. A lot of girls wouldn't do it. So many of our young people leave us for the bright lights these days."

Miss Lucy has finished rewinding and is stuffing microfilm into yellow boxes. She looks at Mrs. Worsham, her face expressionless. From her hand, a strip of microfilm curls and dangles like a tail. She tries to picture herself living in a place with bright lights. The closest she can come is a vision of herself in the parking area of Big Lots at Christmas.

"As for me," says Mrs. Worsham, "if I'd moved to Cincinnati and become a doctor like my high school biology teacher advised instead of taking my degree in library science at Farlanburg State, I wouldn't be standing here today knowing I stayed and made a contribution to my hometown. And I wouldn't have met and married my Edgar. True, I might have met and married some other nice man—"

"One who would pick up his dirty socks," says Shirley. "And not refuse to change his unders."

Mrs. Worsham's face reddens. Hers is the face of a woman who realizes that at some point in the past, following a trivial argument with her husband, she may have sought revenge with her tongue, talked of intimate things, revealed too much. When the redness disappears, she looks wounded but infinitely wiser. "Like I said," she says, curtly, "another man might have been a little easier to take care of, but he wouldn't have been my Edgar. Not as sweet, not as loyal, not as—"

"Edgar," says Shirley.

"Yes," says Mrs. Worsham. "Not as Edgar. And where would I be now?"

"In Cincinnati picking up after someone named Carl," says Shirley. She laughs.

Mrs. Worsham glances at Miss Lucy, sticks out her chin, then turns her attention to her plant, where there is hope. Sarcasm and cynicism are traits that should not be encouraged, she often says. Sarcasm and cynicism have no more place in a library than foul language, bare feet, or shirtless chests.

By the time Miss Lucy finishes with the microfilm, Mrs. Worsham has gone to work on her fern in the foyer. Shirley has returned to her class. Shirley teaches people who did not get an education when they were supposed to. They've come to the library because they know they've missed out on something and have been told they'll finally have it when they get their GED.

Miss Lucy sits at her desk and listens. She got her education when she was supposed to, but she knows she missed out on something, too. She would trade her high school diploma for a husband; her degree from Farlanburg State for a houseful of kids.

When she was in high school and college and still susceptible to wild flights of fancy provoked by a silver moon, she would loop her arms around an invisible neck at night and slow dance in her room. He was tall, more than six feet, and with her cheek against his chest, she listened for the beating of a heart. Later, in her bed, she dreamed she was the mother of nine children, and in her dreams her children were all under two. When she walked through the house, they jumped on her legs and clung there, thirsty for love, tenacious as fleas. They gnawed on her knuckles, used her fingers as teething rings. "Want cookies!" they screamed at all hours. Willingly, at midnight, she baked.

She went to elementary school with many of Shirley's students. They were wild and rowdy when she knew them; now they are older and tamed. Armed with sharp pencils and middle-aged determination, they are ready to learn history and conjugate verbs. At last, they see the value in knowing who defeated the Spanish Armada. "Fools! Go home to your families!" Miss Lucy would say to them if she were the teacher.

"How has a sweet girl like you managed to stay single?" Mrs. Worsham used to tease. When Miss Lucy turned thirty, the teasing stopped. "Somewhere along the line, something tragic must have happened," Mrs. Worsham assured her. "I'll bet you loved a boy, and he died. You hear about that sort of thing all the time."

Miss Lucy supposes something tragic could have happened; she just can't remember what or when. She had a few dates in high school, but most of the boys she knew didn't have a car or gas money, and she lived so far out of town. Once, during the summer, she went out with a preacher's son who was visiting at a neighbor's house. He took Miss Lucy to Meacham's Restaurant for a hamburger, then led her back to the car with a pleading look on his sunburnt, slightly swollen face. He drove her up and down Main Street, through the car wash, past the pizza shop, around and around the Dairy Dip so many times that Miss Lucy had the feeling he was trying to wind her up for something, and she grew dizzy from the heat and queasy from the hamburger and asked to be taken home.

Then there was her date with Freddy Bashem. He wasn't a town boy, and he didn't play a sport, but Miss Lucy still liked him. She curled her hair for him and put on a little makeup. She borrowed one of her mother's dresses and raised the hem above the knees. Freddy was supposed to pick her up at noon, but he was late by a couple of hours. He took her to the stock sale, bought her a Coke, and waved to her from across the pen while he and his father bought calves.

Looking back on it, Miss Lucy wonders whether she loved him. If she did, she didn't know it at the time. And Freddy Bashem didn't die because there is a picture of him in Miss Lucy's yearbook, taken during graduation. He sold his father's farm and bought a bakery in Clendenin. About six years ago, Miss Lucy was up that way, and she stopped in and bought a donut from him. He looked older and had put on a lot of weight, but he was friendly and took time to show her pictures of his family. There was nothing especially wrong with Freddy Bashem, Miss Lucy tells herself, but she can't help feeling slightly disappointed that he might have been the "something tragic" in her life.

At three o'clock, Mrs. Worsham brings Miss Lucy a card file and requests the circulation stats. "Everything all set for the party?"

"Got it all under control," says Miss Lucy. It's not a surprise party. No party in Farlanburg ever is. Mrs. Worsham has threatened to retire twice before, but this time she says she means it. "You people are just going to have to learn to get along without me," she has been saying since January. Officially, she does not retire until mid-May, but she wanted her party early so she wouldn't be tempted to back out.

Mrs. Worsham frowns. "I hope you didn't go to too much trouble."

Miss Lucy dismisses the notion with a wave of her hand. When Mrs. Worsham wanders over to her own desk, Miss Lucy goes downstairs and phones Jack at the deli to remind him about the dip.

"One crab. One onion. And don't forget the vegetable tray."

"Gotcha," says Jack.

"What about the cake?"

"Cake's fine. Don't worry none about the cake. I ain't seen it, but Dovey says she's got it done. Turns 'em out perfect every time."

"It's no big thing," says Miss Lucy.

"I reckon not," says Jack.

"Just a little get-together. Our way of saying good-bye."

Miss Lucy applies a crumpled tissue to her nose, which has a tendency to drip this time of year. "Would it be too much trouble to have all the food over here by a quarter till? The party's at four, but I'd like to make sure we have plenty of time. If that's not too much of a problem."

"No problem," says Jack. "You got'er."

Miss Lucy dabs at her nose once more, then goes back upstairs. She sits at her desk, intending to work on the stats, but she has trouble concentrating. Her desk is remarkably free from clutter. A small, yellow pot filled with dry dirt sits on the left, near the back. Once, it contained a begonia—a gift from Mrs. Worsham, whose own desk resembles an oasis. "Your desk is a clue to your personality," Mrs. Worsham explained when she gave Miss Lucy the plant. "You don't want people to think you have no personality, do you?"

On the opposite side of her desk, for balance, is a photograph in a gold frame—a gift Shirley gave her at the library Christmas party. Miss Lucy picks it up and looks at it. In the photograph, a man, woman, and child are holding hands and running through a field. It could be a wheat field. Miss Lucy cannot tell. She has never been up on her grains. "You're supposed to take that picture out and put your own pictures in," Shirley reminded her when a month had passed and Miss Lucy showed no inclination to remove the models from the frame. "Family pictures, for heaven's sake."

The people in the photograph are beautiful, with honey-colored hair, and long, lovely necks exposed to the sun and wind. Miss Lucy cannot imagine a reason for their running. Perhaps a combine is closing in behind them, threatening to separate flesh from bone. Whatever is after them is coming from behind, though, because the photographer has left a generous amount of space for them to run into, and in doing so, he has given them a future. Lately, Miss Lucy has had a feeling that she, too, is being pursued. But whatever is after her is sneaky and has positioned itself in front of her. It stands, big as a mountain, between her and next week.

"God is testing you," Brother Bennett said when Miss Lucy tried to explain the feeling to him over the phone last Sunday. Brother Bennett is the preacher at Miss Lucy's church. He is a pale, humble-faced man whose quiet sermons are full of talk about shepherds and sheep. He baptized Miss Lucy when she was ten, but other than shaking her hand each week and saying, "May the grace and glory of the Father shine upon you and give you peace," he hasn't had to say much to her since. Still, she thought it might help to talk to him.

She wanted to wait until her father was napping. He lay in his bed in the living room, watching a bass fishing tournament on TV. His foot had snaked its way from under the covers. The ankle was swollen more than usual, the skin, plum-colored and cheesy between the toes.

"Your foot worries me, Daddy."

He reached down and covered it without taking his eyes off the TV. Hidden by blankets, his body seemed flattened, as though he were melting into the bed. When Miss Lucy lifted the covers to check his foot, he kicked feebly at the side of her head. "Stop that!" she said, grabbing his shin. She inspected his foot, then tucked the sheet and covers in at the baseboard. "First thing tomorrow morning, I'm calling one of those new doctors up at the clinic. Fuss and fume all you want. You keep fooling with Doc Harkins, you're gonna lose another leg."

He looked at her, then rolled onto his side, his foot sticking up like a fin as it traveled the width of the bed. "Go to hell. I ain't going to no clinic," he said. Later, he ordered a cup of warm buttermilk. He drank it, then dropped the cup onto the floor. Miss Lucy sat on the couch and watched him settle into sleep. When his breathing was deep and regular, she picked up the phone from the coffee table and dialed Brother Bennett's number. She pulled the kinks and curls out of the cord, stretched it until it reached into the bathroom, then went in, sat down on the commode, and shut the door.

"I can't stand much more of this," she said. She heard a squeaking sound as Brother Bennett shifted in his chair.

"What you're feeling is perfectly normal for a woman in your situation."

Miss Lucy tore off a piece of toilet paper and blew her nose. "Then I want out of my situation."

"Have faith in Him," said Brother Bennett. "He never gives us more than we can handle."

"How do you know?" said Miss Lucy. "Isn't it possible that God is old and forgetful like Doc Harkins? Maybe He overestimates tolerance levels. Gives big red pills to people who ought to have little blue ones."

"Lucy, Lucy," Brother Bennett said, sadly. She could sense his disapproval moving like a clot through the cables, from pole to pole, its weight sagging the wires.

Miss Lucy picks up her pencil and sighs. She stares at the book cards in front of her and makes a half-hearted attempt to tally. The wall clock emits a grinding sound, and she looks up. Her desk is next to a window. Outside, the world is new and pale: the sky, a soft blue; the leaves, still shy and curled. Sunlight filters through the trees. The rays dapple her wrists and fingers.

With the exception of Shirley's students, there are no patrons in the library. There are seldom patrons in the library, despite the fact that the library does its best to find some.

"Read six books a year and win a free trip to Burger King," a sign in the front window promises. That sign is for adults. A poster in the children's section shows a picture of a bearded, anemic-looking man reading by lamplight. At the bottom of the poster are the words: "Abraham Lincoln loved books."

"Abraham Lincoln was kweer," a sly, anonymous Farlanburger has penciled in. The people of Farlanburg do not like books. Or libraries. Libraries remind them of school days and Civil War reports, of a time when they first wanted to be somebody besides themselves and discovered they could not.

When Miss Lucy was in high school, she knew people who wanted to be movie stars, pilots, or mercenaries. She and her small circle of friends did not lean in such directions themselves. The year she graduated, her yearbook entry, like many others, said, "Future: Homemaker." Not an ambitious choice by today's standards, she knows. Not an impossible one, she thought at the time. Life was like a trip to the Piggly Wiggly, she assumed in those days. You went in with a vague idea of what you wanted, followed the arrows up and down the aisles, and emerged, like everyone else, with a full cart.

To date, Farlanburg has produced no movie stars, pilots, or mercenaries. It has turned out some secretaries, teachers, truck drivers, and a couple of librarians. When she was younger, Miss Lucy used to imagine leaving town. She pictured herself out on the bypass, thumb out, truck wind whipping her hair. In her second year of college, she started to work part time at the library. When she graduated, Mrs. Worsham asked if she'd like to stay on, full time. Miss Lucy felt lucky to have an offer. She accepted, boxed up her belongings, and moved into town.

She had a cousin who lived in Knoxville. She didn't know him well, but at reunions he seemed happier than anyone else. Miss Lucy planned to work in Farlanburg a couple of years, save her money, and move to Knoxville. The following spring, her mother died.

"Your Daddy's lucky to have you close by," out-of-state relatives, who came home for the funeral, said. "Will you be moving back out to the farm?"

Miss Lucy stayed in her apartment, a difficult decision, and for the first time in her life, she felt alive and in charge. A year later, her father lost his leg. One evening, after visiting him in the hospital, she read a letter in the county paper. The letter was written by a seventy-six-year-old man, a retired auto worker, a former Farlanburger who had moved to Indiana. His subscription was about to expire, and he wanted to renew it. His note appeared as a letter to the editor. "Dear Sirs," the note began. "Enclosed is twelve dollars to pay for my subscription another year. There is nothing like keeping up with hometown news. Forty-five years I have been here in Indiana, worked all over this great country of ours before that. I am a veteran of the Second World War. It's a funny thing about my hometown. Wherever I've gone, a little place of Farlanburg has gone with me." The letter ended with a poem:

No matter how far I roam,
Farlanburg will be home.
God bless you one and all, dear friends,
And a special hello to my wife's brother, Mr. Harlan Avery.

Miss Lucy clipped the letter from the paper and carried it with her for several days until she understood what it meant. There was a message in it for her, and the message, she finally decided, was that regardless of how far you travel, there are some things that simply cannot be outrun.

So, on afternoons like this one, when she has nothing better to do, she sits at her desk, stares out the window and watches former classmates trudge up and down the streets. Like her, they have grown up and out and older. They are the parents of tiny pink and blue bundles nestled among the celery and Rice Krispies in the grocery carts. They have six-year-olds, who run at full throttle up and down the aisles.

These are the people Miss Lucy has envied. But lately, even that has changed. "Envy is at the heart of most misery," Brother Bennett said in his sermon, Wednesday night. "Make a list of the people you envy most, try to determine what those people have in common, then strive to develop those characteristics in yourself." Miss Lucy made a list. On her list are her mother, her Aunt Opal, and a high school friend named Gloria. The characteristic those people have in common is that they're dead.

At 3:30, Shirley finishes with her students. There is no summary, no wrap-up, no sense that anything is winding down. Shirley simply stops talking and waits. For a moment, her students sit there and blink. When they see that nothing more is coming, they pick up their books and go. They are silent as they leave the library, their faces serious, stunned by how much they know.

"Good-bye. See you on Monday," Mrs. Worsham calls to them. "Those people inspire me," she says when Shirley's last student is gone.

"Strange," says Shirley. "They depress the hell out of me."

Mrs. Worsham gives Shirley a reproachful glance. "They remind me of just how lucky I am. I look at them and that's how I know I've been blessed."

Jack calls to say he's on his way with the food. Miss Lucy and Shirley go downstairs to help him carry it in. The basement is stale, harsh under fluorescent lights. Zebras, hippopotamuses, and exotic birds decorate the Story Hour wall. At the other end of the room, balloon clusters hang from the ceilings, and two large pink-and-white floral arrangements sit at each end of a table. Miss Lucy decorated early that morning. She thought the flowers might droop or the balloons lose air. They haven't.

Miss Lucy takes pink paper plates, cups, and napkins from the kitchen cabinets and arranges them in rows on the table while Shirley pours punch from a plastic container into the library's glass serving bowl. Jack shows up with the vegetable tray. "H-e-e-e-r-e-'s Jack!" he says. "Where do you want it?"

Miss Lucy points to the center table. "Would you mind putting it over there?"

Shirley goes outside to carry in the cake. Jack puts the vegetables on the table and then stands with his hands hanging awkwardly at his sides. "Nice," he says, as he surveys the room. He is a stout little man who looks as if he has eaten as many cakes as he's baked.

Miss Lucy inspects the vegetable tray. "Where's the dip?"

Jack frowns. He bends, puts his hands on his knees, and stares at the tray as if he expects to discover something hidden under the radishes. "Damn," he says.

Miss Lucy inhales slowly and releases air through her mouth. "I guess we'll have to get along without it."

"Where does this go?" says Shirley, who has returned with the cake.

Miss Lucy nods toward the kitchen.

Jack shrugs. "Dip ain't all that good for you anyway."

"That's exactly what they say about retirement!" says

Mrs. Worsham, who descends the stairs followed by several Friends of the Library. "Jack Pearson? Is that you? I thought I recognized your voice." Mrs. Worsham smiles and shakes Jack's hand as though she hasn't seen him in a year. She has applied fresh lipstick, Miss Lucy notices. Her lips are coral and match the punch. She presses her palms together and shakes her head as she looks around the basement. "You girls shouldn't have."

Shirley sticks her head out the kitchen door. "You're right," she says, winking at Miss Lucy. Everyone laughs.

Warren Arganbright from City Council and five members of the Library Board arrive. Warren, a retired Army colonel, much sought-after as a speaker by the civic groups in town, is known for his spit-and-polish appearance and eloquent turns of phrase. This afternoon, he smiles broadly as he embraces Mrs. Worsham. "Never let it be said that I passed up an opportunity to spend an afternoon with lovely ladies," he says. Again, everyone laughs. "What'd he say? What'd he say?" Margaret Jones asks.

Miss Lucy nudges the guests toward the refreshment table. "There's plenty of food and punch," she says. "You all just help yourselves."

Someone taps her on the shoulder. It's Jack. He winks and motions for her to follow him to the kitchen. "I want you to see the cake," he says.

In the kitchen, Shirley leans against the counter, smoking a cigarette. "You're not supposed to do that in here," Jack whispers. He points to a "No Smoking" sign on the wall.

Shirley stares at the sign. "What the hell," she says. "Is this a party or not?"

Jack removes a single candle, which has been taped like a small torpedo to the side of the box. "You're gonna like it," he says. He carefully unfastens more tape and lifts the lid. "Ta da!" He watches Miss Lucy's face.

The cake is white with three layers, decorated with pink icing roses, perfectly sculpted. The inscription, written in green, loops and curls like an elegant vine across the top. "TODAY IS THE FIRST DAY OF THE REST OF YOUR LIFE."

Miss Lucy stares at the cake. "What is this?"

"The cake," says Jack.

Miss Lucy shakes her head. "This is not what I ordered. This is not what I told you to put on there."

"You didn't tell me nothing," says Jack.

Shirley smiles and flicks the ash from her cigarette.

"You said it was a retirement cake. That's all you said. You didn't say nothing about what you wanted on it." Jack's fleshy ears have changed from pink to red. He folds his arms and plants his feet farther apart as though preparing to defend his cake. "Dovey saw this in a book and thought you folks'd like it. She put the same thing on Evert Ramsey's cake last year when he retired, and he didn't complain none." Jack frowns at Miss Lucy. He blinks his little black eyes and looks at Shirley.

Shirley makes a disapproving sound with her tongue. She inhales, opens her mouth, and a smoke ring emerges. It floats upward in front of her face, then dissolves in midair.

"Jesus H. Christ," says Jack. "Try to do something nice for someone, and this is the thanks you get." He pulls the bill from his shirt pocket, lays it on the counter, and leaves.

Shirley stubs her cigarette out in the sink. "No big deal. It's just a corny saying. If you don't mention it, no one'll even notice."

Miss Lucy shakes her head and looks at the cake. "That's not the point," she says, bleakly.

Shirley swipes through a clump of icing stuck to the top of

the box, then licks her finger. "Ok. What is the point?"

Miss Lucy stares at the cake, then turns her back to it. "It's a message. Just like that old man's letter."

"What old man?" says Shirley.

"A toast!" someone shouts.

"Come on," says Shirley, but Miss Lucy doesn't move. Shirley takes her arm, and Miss Lucy allows herself to be led toward the party. Someone puts an empty cup in her hand and Miss Lucy, like everyone around her, holds the cup aloft as though she is waiting for something to fall out of the air.

Warren Arganbright's deep voice rises above the chatter. "To Mrs. Worsham," he says, solemnly. "May her retirement be as long and productive as her association with this library, and may she continue in good health and in happiness among her many friends in our little town." Mrs. Worsham's eyes fill as her friends drink to her. Kyle Jamison presses forward and presents her with a dozen red roses, and when Shirley carries out the cake, tears spill down Mrs. Worsham's cheeks and hang from her chin.

Later, when the cake has been cut, the guests served, and the punch stands at low tide, Mrs. Worsham works her way through the crowd to Miss Lucy. "I have a little something for you," she whispers. She pulls a small white envelope from behind her back and presses it into Miss Lucy's hand. "It's nothing much, and it wouldn't mean a thing to anyone except us, but I really want you to have it." Mrs. Worsham dabs at her eyes with a handkerchief and hugs Miss Lucy. "Don't open it until you're alone."

Shirley helps Miss Lucy clean up. They stack tables, fold chairs, take down balloons, and scrape leftovers into the garbage. "See, you got all worked up over the cake for nothing," says Shirley. "I don't think anyone even read it. It could've said, 'Today is the last day of your life,' and these people wouldn't have noticed. To them it all tastes the same."

When they finish, Shirley gets her sweater and purse. "I guess that about takes care of it," she says.

Miss Lucy nods. She picks up a white balloon and stares into it as though it were a crystal ball. "I hear you're leaving us."

Shirley is putting on her sweater. She stops, looks at Miss Lucy a moment, then laughs. "If you want to look at it that way," she says, poking her arm through a sleeve. "I thought I was leaving Russ."

"Same thing."

"Not in my book," says Shirley. She buttons her sweater and digs her car keys from her purse.

Miss Lucy hugs the balloon to her chest. "We'll miss you."

"Come visit," says Shirley. "Better yet, move. We have libraries in New Jersey, you know."

Miss Lucy twists the string on her balloon. "I can't," she says. "My father."

"Sure you can. We have fathers in New Jersey, too."

"You don't understand," says Miss Lucy.

Shirley opens the basement door and winks. "Bull's eye," she says. "You're right."

Miss Lucy locks up. She checks to make sure the basement door is shut, then goes upstairs and turns off all the lights. She pauses in the foyer at the front of the library and removes the envelope from her skirt pocket. Inside are two heavy keys on a gold-colored chain. There is a note. "Dear Lucy, I know you already have a set of keys, but I wanted you to have these. They don't fit the new lock because they were given to me thirty years ago when I first started to work at the library. I hope your new position will bring you as much happiness as it has brought me. With fondest regards, Mrs. Worsham."

Miss Lucy puts the note and keys back in the envelope and drops the envelope into her purse. She pulls the door shut, and as she steps into evening on Main Street, a warm wind lifts and plays with her hair. Hopscotch squares decorate the sidewalks; the smell of freshly cut grass lingers in the air. She shifts her purse from shoulder to shoulder as she heads toward home.

When she turns the corner onto Stringer Street, she spots her landlady digging in the yard. Though Mrs. Tucker is a couple of years older than Miss Lucy's father, she still gardens. She's wearing a sun hat and floral print dress, and with her back to Miss Lucy, she is as bright as any flower.

"It's spring," Miss Lucy calls over the fence, so she won't scare her. Mrs. Tucker is hard of hearing, and at the sound of a voice, she stares at her lilac bush as if she thinks it has spoken. "Oh!" she cries, jumping when Miss Lucy comes through the gate. "Did you say something?"

At the window above the garage, the curtains move slightly, and Miss Lucy sees her father's face behind the glass. "I said, 'It's spring!' " she shouts.

Mrs. Tucker smiles vaguely. "Yes," she says after awhile. She moves closer to Miss Lucy. "I took a bunch of green onions up to your Daddy at noon. He told me his foot's paining him pretty bad. You better get someone to take a look at it."

Miss Lucy nods and shuts her eyes. When she opens them, Mrs. Tucker is staring at the sky. Miss Lucy looks up and sees a jet.

"You ever been on one?" says Mrs. Tucker.

Miss Lucy shakes her head.

"I have. Two years ago. I rode one when I went out to see Teddy and his family in California. You remember my boy Teddy, don't you? I bet you went to school with him."

"Not really," says Miss Lucy. "He was a few years ahead of me."

Mrs. Tucker watches Miss Lucy's lips until they stop moving. She is quiet a moment, her cheeks working in and out. "We was good to him," she says, frowning. "I don't know what we did to make him want to move so far from home." She reaches out and wraps her fingers around Miss Lucy's arm. "Your Daddy's lucky having you right here to take care of him. I guess it's different with girls."

A cool wind sweeps through the yard. The jet cuts across the sky, leaving a silver scar behind it, and Miss Lucy watches, hypnotized by the glint of sun on the wings. For a moment, she is flying, not just a passenger but a pilot, while far below her, a daughter goes inside to fix her father's supper and a landlady leans on her hoe and envies an old man's luck.

Baby Luv

My sister Nedra has a dead baby. I'm eleven, and I'm alive; it doesn't seem fair. I sit in the backseat of Dewdie's Pontiac convertible and watch the sunlight slice like a golden knife through a hole in the roof of the car. Dewdie is Nedra's husband. He's wanted a Pontiac convertible all his life, and now that he's on regular at the shoe plant, he can afford one. Once, I was mad that it was used and had a hole in its top. Not anymore. It's funny the things you'll forgive a person after his baby has died.

In the front seat, Nedra holds the baby in her arms and waits for Dewdie to get his things and come out of the motel. Dewdie's been sleeping there for the past two days waiting for the baby to die. It's not a Howard Johnson. It never is.

Nedra's eyes are swollen like she's been bee stung, and her mascara has run so that it looks like someone laid a little rubber on her face. She's bowled over with grief, Dewdie said, and I'm supposed to leave her alone. She doesn't look like she should be left alone.

I'm not supposed to look at the baby either. Dewdie didn't say that. He didn't have to. I read once that it's good manners not to stare at people who are crippled or naked or dead. That's OK by me. There are some things I don't want to see.

A pair of Dewdie's muddy shoes are sticking out from under the seat. I scrunch down and shut my eyes. I fish the shoes out with my toes and try them on to help pass the time.

Sitting in a Pontiac convertible in front of a no-TV motel with a dead baby in the car isn't normal. I know that. Some things people have to tell me, and some things I just naturally know. Nothing about us is normal—Dewdie, Nedra, Mammaw, and me. We eat leftover chili for breakfast, fight too much, and watch preaching on Saturday night on TV.

We don't even die like other people, the right way, at four o'clock in the morning before anyone else gets up. I guess Baby Luv couldn't help when he did it though. That's what we called him. The baby. His name was Delbert Herschel Denny, but Nedra and Dewdie called him Baby Luv after some Diana Ross record they used to dance to. They spelled it like the diapers to be original.

Baby Luv had been sick and in and out of the hospital a lot since Nedra had him. The doctors gave him a health score right after he was born and said he was a "ten," like in that movie, I guess. Nedra was real proud and said she felt like she'd finally done something right for once.

Nedra has flubbed up on a lot of things during her life. She married Bobby Sutphin and divorced him. She didn't finish beauty school either. So when the doctors came in her room that day after she'd had Baby Luv and told her that her baby had problems, she thought they were joking. "Would it be my kid if it didn't?" Nedra said. When she saw they weren't kidding, she was worried.

Dewdie wasn't. "Nobody in my family has kids who are less than a nine," he bragged.

By six o'clock that evening, Baby Luv was real sick. Mammaw and I went back to the hospital to be with Nedra. We've always been a family who does things together even if we do fight a lot while we're doing them.

Nedra was taking it real hard. So was Dewdie. "What did you do to him?" Dewdie was saying to Nedra when we walked in.

"Do to who?" Mammaw wanted to know.

Dewdie ignored us and went right on talking to Nedra. "My brother's kids are fine. My sister's kids are fine. My kid ain't. By God, I want to know why!" Dewdie said.

"Let me hit him," I begged Mammaw. I would've, too, if Nedra had given me the go-ahead, but she just turned her back to all of us and stared at the wall. A nurse came in and said we were all tired and under a lot of stress and stuff and that was the reason we were acting that way. I knew better. If I'd heard Mammaw say it once, I'd heard her say it a thousand times that she's never known a Denny what wouldn't kick you when you were down, and Dewdie was no exception.

Anyway, Baby Luv was born sick, and he stayed that way the whole six months he was alive. The doctors poked him full of holes, but they never did find out what was wrong with him. One of them said he was sure whatever it was didn't happen in his hospital but happened while the baby was still inside Nedra.

Dewdie really pointed his finger at Nedra then. He said Nedra'd probably smoked cigarettes on the sly just to spite him and pay him back for some picky little thing he might've done like the time he took Janice Kimble home and fixed the radiator on her car for free.

That made Nedra cry. She said she would *never* have done anything to hurt her own baby. I stood up for her and said I knew it was so. "I have never smelled a cigarette on my sister's breath," I told Dewdie, settling it then and there.

Nedra and I aren't friends like I've read that sisters ought to be. Mammaw says it's because Nedra is seven years older, but I think it's because Nedra is Nedra, and I'm me. But I was the one who was with her when her baby died. You'd have thought it would've been Mammaw or Dewdie, but no, it was me. In a way, I'm glad because I think Nedra saw that people don't have to be old enough to shave their legs to care.

Dewdie was at the motel sleeping, and Mammaw had gone home to get some rest. The nurse had let me in the room to be with Nedra and the baby for a little while. I wasn't supposed to be in there, so I was being real quiet and doing my best to look honest. The quickest way to get thrown out of a hospital, I have learned, is to look like you are sneaky and would lie about your age.

Baby Luv was asleep in this bed that looked like a hot house where they grow winter tomatoes. He had needles in his arms, and his chest was going in and out and in and out. I felt sorry for him and wondered why he was in there instead of me. I don't think it has anything to do with how many lies you've told or how mean you've been.

I walked over to say hi to him and peeked though the bars at the side. Nedra said not to touch him, so I just looked. I wasn't going to hurt him. I just wanted him to know that I was there. Some people say babies don't know one face from another. They're wrong.

Suddenly, Baby Luv opened his eyes and smiled at me. "Guess what?" I said to Nedra. "He smiled when he saw *I* was here."

Nedra stared at me, then came over and looked at the baby. When she started yelling for a nurse, I thought I'd said something to make her mad. I wanted her to be quiet so the nurse wouldn't come in and put me out of there. "He smiles a whole lot more for you! I've never seen a baby smile so much for his mama!" I said, trying to make it better. Then I looked at Baby Luv and saw that Nedra was yelling because of him. His chest, which had been going in and out and in and out, was going in but taking a long time to come back out.

A nurse came in and checked him and told us not to worry. "He's fine," she said. She said it was the medicine they were giving him that was making him act that way. I looked at Nedra to see if we should believe her.

"Are you sure?" Nedra said.

"I'm sure," said the nurse.

What could we say?

The nurse went out, and Nedra stood there with her eyes glued to the baby. My eyes were glued to Nedra. I imagined a triangle between us. Pretty soon, the in and out was just in again, and Baby Luv began to make a noise that sounded like he had a chicken bone stuck in his throat. Nedra started screaming again. That same nurse ran in and shoved me out of the way. She took one look at Baby Luv and said she'd better get a doctor. She brought back a lot of them. Before long, there were people running all over the place.

They had more needles, and they stuck one into Baby Luv's chest. He wasn't making the chicken-bone noise anymore. They started squeezing on him then, and Nedra let them. I wanted to stop them, but my feet wouldn't move. I put my hands over my ears and heard someone screaming again. A man grabbed me and pulled me into the hall before I figured out that this time the screaming was coming from me.

"Stay!" he said, like you do to a dog, and I said I wouldn't. He just stood there staring at me for a minute the way people do when they're trying to figure out how much sense you've got. "If you *really* love your sister, you'll stay out here in the hall where you belong," he said. I heard the way he said "really." He had no right to say it that way. Like he was accusing me of something. I waited till he left, then I began to cry.

I sat there watching the clock by myself for awhile. Finally, I got up and went back in the room. No one seemed to notice. The doctors were still doing things to Baby Luv, but they acted like they were just waiting for someone to tell them it was OK to stop. Nedra was holding Baby Luv's hand and crying and saying over and over, "Let him go. Let him go." No one was listening to her. Finally, one of them did, and they all just backed away. Nedra told them to get their needles out of her baby, and when they did, she picked him up.

"I hope you're not going to hold the hospital responsible for this," the nurse said. Nedra just stood there with her eyes shut and said she didn't hold nobody responsible for nothing.

Some people have said our family doesn't have a lot of class. I, myself, have thought the same about Nedra more than once. But I knew then that some people were wrong just like I'd been wrong so long about Nedra, and I told that nurse so. "You're lucky my sister has class," I said. "If it'd been me you said that to, I'd'a floored you."

Nedra gave me some money and a phone number and told me to call Dewdie. A man said I could use the phone at the nurses' desk. "No thank you," I said. "I can pay."

When Dewdie came to the hospital, he reached for Baby Luv, but Nedra held on to him and wouldn't let Dewdie have him. Dewdie put his arms around her then, and they stood there a minute with their heads down. After a while, we started to leave the room with our baby, and that's when it happened. That same nurse started patting Nedra's shoulder like you do when you like someone or are trying to bring them around to your way of thinking. She told Nedra we couldn't do it that way.

"What way?" Dewdie wanted to know, and the nurse said we couldn't just walk out of a hospital holding on to a dead baby.

"Why not?" said Dewdie.

"You just can't, that's all," the nurse said, frowning. I don't think she knew the answer though, because she went out in the hall and brought a doctor in to explain.

"It's quite simple, Mr. Denny," the doctor said. He was a little man who looked like he'd spent his life washing his hands. "You'd like to know why your baby died, wouldn't you?"

"Don't see where it makes much difference," Dewdie said. "He's dead."

Dewdie and the doctor stood there looking at each other, and I knew Dewdie would get the best of him like he does every time he and Nedra play "stare down."

"We'll need to do an autopsy, Mr. Denny," the doctor finally said.

Nedra started screaming and saying that nobody was going to cut on her baby.

"Shut up and let me handle it," Dewdie said, then he turned around and said Nedra was right. "I'm taking my baby out of here, and I'd like to see the man big enough to stop me."

I have to admit I've never liked Dewdie much, partly because he's a Denny and partly because of the way he mouths off to Nedra all the time. But I liked him then. I think Mammaw would've too if she'd been there to hear him.

Dewdie took charge like a man who's used to being that way. He got on the phone and called long distance to Mammaw, then he called long distance to the courthouse in Badden County where we live and talked to Harold Catron, who knows about autopsies and such things. Harold told Dewdie that no one has to have an autopsy if he doesn't want one unless there are suspicions of foul play. "The only foul thing about any of this is what I'm going to say if these people don't get out of my way and let me take my baby home," Dewdie said.

When Dewdie hung up the phone, the doctor nodded at the others and said, "Let 'em leave." They stood there staring at each other while Dewdie and Nedra and the baby and me walked out of that room and down those long halls and into the afternoon sun.

That's the way we did it. The next thing I know, we're sitting in front of the motel waiting for Dewdie to pay. "Wish he'd hurry up," Nedra says, and we both stare at the motel office where Dewdie is talking to a bald man who's taking his time like this is just any ordinary day and there's not a dead baby waiting outside his motel in the heat.

On the way home, we're quiet, except for Nedra, who sings to Baby Luv and arranges his arms and legs so they'll get stiff in a pretty position, the way they do if you have it done in a funeral home. I listen to her sing and think how glad I am Dewdie fixed the muffler on the car last week.

We stop by Horton's to get a casket. Bertis Horton raises rabbits to eat and works in his daddy's funeral home.

"You couldn't 'a' picked a better one for the price," Bertis says as he helps Dewdie load the casket in the trunk of the car. The car lid won't close, and Dewdie has to tie it down with string.

Bertis pretends to help, but I see him staring at Nedra. I know what he's up to. He wants to see what's in the front seat. He's still standing there when we drive away.

By the time we get home, a mound of fresh, red dirt is piled high like an ant hill on the ridge back of the cellar house. Mammaw says Willard Pyles deserves the thanks for the digging, and, sure enough, there stands Willard in the backyard, drinking a glass of ice water, dripping sweat, and mumbling that he likes to help when he can.

"Thanks," says Dewdie, and Willard says forget it.

Nedra takes Baby Luv up to the room above the cellar house where she and Dewdie have lived since they got married. Mammaw goes up. "She's bathing the baby. She's going to pack some of his toys in with him," Mammaw tells me when she comes back down.

"Why?" I ask her. "He's not going to be able to play with them."

"Hush your mouth," Mammaw says. "What a selfish thing to say."

Dewdie and Willard carry the casket up the hill. After a while, they come back down, and Nedra and Mammaw go up. It's strange how they all seem to know what they're doing like they've practiced it sometime before. Mammaw has her black Bible, and Nedra's carrying something wrapped in a blanket. I know it's Baby Luv.

When they come off the hill, Mammaw looks at me. "If you're planning on seeing him again, now's the time to do it," she says. "You want me to go with you?"

I shake my head.

"Pull the covers away from his face if you want to," Nedra says. "He looks just as natural as can be. Like he's sleeping or something." I look at her, and she looks at me, and there are tears running down her face. Nedra has never liked for me to see her cry. Now it doesn't seem to matter.

As I climb alone up the hill, I think this must've been what it was like for Baby Luv when he was dying, except he floated instead of walked, and he wasn't out of breath when he got where he was going. I wonder if it hurts to die? At the top, I walk between the humps that are Grandpa and Grandma Whitson and then go left past Uncle Holly. I kneel in front of the open casket and peep into the grave.

I don't pull back the blue quilt Mammaw made for Baby Luv not long after he was born. Instead, I sit there for a long time looking out over the valley, past the rusted tin roofs of the house and cellar below, and I remember the time Nedra told me this was her "jumping-off" spot, her favorite spot in the whole world because she could come up here and pretend to fly.

When I go back down, Willard is gone. Nedra and Dewdie are sitting in the swing under the maple tree, and they're holding hands like they used to. Today, Dewdie loves Nedra, Mammaw loves Dewdie, and I think they even love me. Everything is so wrong that, for once, everything is all right.

Leona Miller has been there and left a ham, and Cora Lockhard called to say she's bring over some pies. Our table already sags under the weight of our neighbors' food.

Mammaw is in the kitchen sampling cakes. I smell ham warming in the oven. I think it's awful to eat when someone's dead.

"Is this it?" I say.

Mammaw looks at the loaded table, then frowns at me. She thinks I'm talking about the food. "There's enough here for anyone, missy," she says. "You need to stop being so picky about what you eat."

I shake my head. My mouth begins to pucker. "I'm not going to eat," I say. "The rest of you can do what you want, but I'm not going to eat."

Mammaw hollers out the screen door for Dewdie and Nedra to get their shovels and do what they've got to do because supper will soon be cold. She takes the ham from the oven and gets a knife. "People got to eat," she says, as she begins to slice.

Structural Changes

Eva Duncan was bent over the potato bin in her cellar, sorting last year's crop according to degree of shrivel and length of sprout, when she heard a low, growling sound that could have been her stomach or distant thunder, but, on second thought, could have been the dogs warning her she had company coming, in which case she planned to stay in her cellar and hide. Spring was a busy time of year for Eva. She had flower beds to sow, an early garden to plant. Too much visiting during the week rather than on Sundays, as God had intended, was what was wrong with the world these days. Potato in hand, she stood with her good ear toward the door and listened.

She tried to remember what the weather had been like when she came in: sunny, not a cloud in the sky as best she could recall, but at her age, she couldn't recall, so she wouldn't have been surprised to poke her head out the door and have it knocked off by a chunk of ice from a hailstorm.

She'd been hoping for a couple days of nice weather so her daughter's friend from college could come by and patch the roof on her house. During the winter, it had sprung several leaks. Rain poured through holes in the rusty tin, collected in dark pools in the attic, then seeped through the upstairs ceilings, leaving brown water marks that ruined the paint and made Eva feel as though someone were spitting at her in her bed at night. Pots and pans covered the floors, and water plinked and ploinked in them during storms until she couldn't sleep.

Eva reached for the light she'd hung on a nail above the potato bin and was careful not to trip over the extension cord as she tiptoed toward the front of her cellar. Halfway there, at the point where the stone wall made an L allowing her to see the door and the lemon-colored rectangle of sunlight, she made a bet with herself that the noise she'd heard had been a car or truck. She checked her watch: 2:15. It was nowhere near time for Margaret to be coming home from work and school.

Margaret was her daughter, and they lived together on a farm that had been in Eva's family for years. Eva was the fourth generation to live there. It was her dream that Margaret, an only child, would stay and be the fifth. She hoped Margaret would remarry and have a couple of babies before her ovaries turned sour. At thirty-eight, she didn't have much time.

Eva and her daughter didn't get much company during the spring. Their house was off the highway up a hollow, and visitors had to cross a creek to get there. The creek was highest this time of year, the narrow dirt road full of ruts and mudholes. The only people who would bring a car through such a loblolly would be a salesman or Jehovah's Witness, and Eva had nothing to say to either. She stopped just inside the cellar entrance, listened, then stuck out her hand and gently closed the door.

She had just dropped several rotten potatoes into a bucket and was thinking she'd feed them to the hogs, then remembered—oh! she didn't have hogs, there hadn't been hogs on the farm in years, not since Lloyd died, a farm without hogs, how depressing!—when she heard the growling sound again, only louder, and the dogs began to bark. "Cussed things!" said Eva. She wiped her hands on her apron and was about to go outside to have a look around when the quart jars of green beans and tomato juice on the shelves started to clink and rattle. One fell off and splattered, sending green beans and shards of glass skating over the floor.

Eva ducked and screamed then wound her arms around the posts of the potato bin and clung to it. "Have mercy on me a sinner!" she pleaded. She knew now what was happening. She'd studied it in her Bible since childhood. "And, lo, the sun became black as sackcloth of hair, and the moon became as blood," the Word said. Reading about it was one thing; actual participation, another. She hadn't felt such panic since the winter Lloyd died and left her with fifty head of cattle and no hay.

She shut her eyes and tried to pray, but the only words that came to mind were practical and unholy: "Not like this, please not like this, potato dirt on my hands, all alone, Lord, with spiders and blacksnakes in my cellar." What she really wanted was time, just a little more time, and if she couldn't have that, she wanted Margaret. What if they couldn't find each other later in the crowd and confusion above?

Gradually, Eva loosened her grip on the post and sank to a kneeling position on the floor. She waited for the blinding flash that would take her, waited on the cold stone slab until her blood turned to slush and her legs felt like popsicles, and while she was waiting, the awful thought occurred to her that Margaret might not be among the chosen. "Two women shall be grinding at the mill; the one shall be taken, and the other left," the Good Book said. Margaret hadn't been in the world long enough for her sins to pile up on her like junk in an attic, but it was a fact that Margaret was divorced. She'd run off during her senior year in high school and married Buddy Duffy, lived with him on Spruce Fork one spring and summer, then just showed up as unexpected as frost in Eva's yard one morning. Eva couldn't say she blamed her for leaving him. She didn't think she could stand to live with one of the beardy Duffys herself or anywhere but the homeplace, for that matter. "But what God has joined together, let no man put asunder," she intoned. In her opinion, instructions didn't get any plainer.

And lately, since Margaret had started taking afternoon art classes at the college, she'd been running with a pretty rough crowd. She'd come home more than once with beer on her breath and an acrid, burning smell on her clothes as though some fire inside her flickered but refused to go out. Margaret had been a good girl in high school. Now here she was, old enough to be married and have kids half-grown, acting like a teenager. "She's still my daughter," Eva said. "She may seem tainted on the outside, but she's pure at heart. You don't take her, I ain't going either!"

Eva hoisted herself off the floor and gave her legs time to come to life. When she pushed open the cellar door, the sunlight blinded her and caused her eyes to water. She paused in the doorway and stuck her head out to see what was going on.

Her house—house of her father, Ben, house of her grand-father Lemuel, house of her great-grandfather Ozrow—stood as it had for more than a hundred and thirty years. The up-stairs porches sagged a little, giving the impression the house suffered from progressive curvature of the spine, and after several hard winters, the white paint on the weatherboard siding had lost a little of its luster. But overall, Eva thought her homeplace appeared structurally sound, and she was as happy to find it that way as she would've been to hear that an aged cousin, reported to have passed on to the next world, was, in fact, still hanging around this one. During the years, Eva had come to think of her house as living, and if she'd had occasion to crawl under it, she wouldn't have been surprised to find the sills had put down roots.

Shading her eyes from the sun, she surveyed the yard. The maple trees showed no signs of having had their bark singed. Fire and destruction were part of the plan, she recalled. A third of the earth and the trees would be consumed, but at the moment, she was relieved it wasn't *her* land and *her* timber. Still, as she hurried down the walk toward her house, she was surprised by the lack of any signs of change. One of her dogs, a spotted brute, stuck its head from under the porch and whined. "Hold on," said Eva, "and I'll see what's happening."

In the kitchen, she flipped the radio off the weather band and tuned in to Farlanburg's only station. Bill Simpson, one of the local announcers, was talking about soybeans, school bonds, and earthquakes.

"Earthquakes!" Eva put her hand on the refrigerator for support.

"Mild earthquake," said Bill. "Phone calls from several sec-tions of the county. No damage reported. Probably low on Richard's scale."

"Richard who?" said Eva. She leaned her elbows on the

counter and put her mouth close to the radio. "We don't have earthquakes in these parts. Seventy-six years I've lived on this place, and I've never seen an earthquake."

"Earthquake," repeated Bill Simpson for the benefit of those who had just tuned in.

Eva blinked and stepped back as though he'd sassed her. She bent over and ran her hands along the baseboard beside the stove to see if there'd been damage. Termites, she guessed, from the spongy condition of the wood, but nothing more serious than that. She checked the ceiling in the dining room for new cracks, inspected the wainscoting for recent splits. "Earthquake," she said, frowning, and she moved her mouth as though tasting the sound of it. She'd never been involved in an earthquake, to the best of her knowledge, and the newness of her situation sent her straight to bed.

Eva had wanted to hire Claude Ferguson to fix her roof. He'd done the only work her house had needed since she'd lived in it, and she was partial to him. His prices were fair, she knew his daddy, and he didn't track in mud or cuss. He'd wired the house for electricity in 1956, and Eva had hired him to put a bathroom in the year after that. She asked him to put the bathroom next to the kitchen because the water lines were already there and handy. Lloyd suggested a bathroom might be more appropriate at the end of the downstairs hallway, but Eva was against it. Pictures of her ancestors had hung there for as long as she could remember, and she couldn't bear the thought of them so close to a commode. Besides, a bathroom at the end of the hallway would have meant adding on an extra section to the side of the house, which would have ruined the house's appearance, in Eva's opinion.

"I'll do whatever you want, Miz Duncan," Claude told her, "but my advice to you is not to put your bathroom in your kitchen. You'll lose counter space."

"Not to mention privacy," said Lloyd.

Eva wanted to keep her homeplace just the way it was when it was built. The prospect of a little convenience was not enough to persuade her to participate in the sacrilege of structural changes.

It had been Margaret's idea to hire one of her friends from college to fix the roof. "There's this guy I know in the art department, Mama, who can fix it in no time," Margaret'd said, snapping her fingers. "He's a good worker, he's cheap, and he's real creative. He did some work once for Lily Disney."

"Never heard of her," said Eva. "Gimme Claude."

"Disney," said Margaret. "Walt's wife. This guy did some work on one of their homes in California."

"I ain't got but one home," said Eva, "and I don't want a Mickey Mouse painted on it." Eventually, rather than argue, Eva gave in. She was trying to allow her daughter to make more decisions about the house and farm since one day it would all belong to her—three hundred and fifty acres and a deed to prove it. True, the barn and outbuildings had rotted a little, and the pastureland lay buried under a sea of multiflora rose. But with a little effort, Eva figured, it would take no time to turn the place into a working farm again.

At twenty minutes past five, Eva had been up from her nap long enough to put a pot of soup on for supper. She had just finished sampling it and was trying to remember what ingredients she had used to produce no taste, when she heard someone coming, peeked out the window, and witnessed her new Chrysler K-Car barreling up the road toward the house.

"Slow down!" yelled Eva, pecking on the window glass. She watched as the car flew past the hickory tree at the corner of the yard. As it neared the hump caused by an oversized culvert the county road department had put in, she shut her eyes and lifted her shoulders to soften the impact. She heard a dull thwacking sound as the car hit the hump, then three ka-chung, ka-chung, ka-chunga noises that reminded her of the racket kids make jumping on beds. When she opened her eyes, the car had passed from sight, in front of the house, and she heard tires slinging rocks as her daughter took the sharp curve by the henhouse and wheeled the K-Car into the barnlot.

Six weeks before, Eva had gone halves on the car with Margaret. She'd paid cash out of what was left of her cattle money, and Margaret was supposed to pay her back a little each month. The deal was they would park the car at the mouth of the hollow and walk in and out until the mud dried up. But Margaret had never been one for walking, so the deal only lasted three days.

"Shame on you!" said Eva. "What's the world coming to? People walked everywhere in my day. It certainly never hurt us." Eva had driven the car only one time, down to Miller's grocery and back, and she was beginning to wonder whether it would last long enough to take advantage of the free oil change Tate's Motors had promised.

"I want you to remember, Mama, that it's your car, too," Margaret had said the day they drove it home. "If you don't drive it once in a while, I'll feel like it was nothing but a handout."

In a sense, Eva thought, it was, but she preferred to think

of it as an investment in her daughter's future. Margaret could barely have made payments by herself when she worked full time as a secretary at the courthouse. Now that she only worked part time and took classes at the college, her financial situation was even worse. And by investing in her daughter's future, Eva had the strange sensation she was investing in her own. She did not want her only child to go off and work as a secretary in Detroit, Michigan, or Cleveland, Ohio, which was what Margaret, when she got in one of her moods, threatened to do.

Eva had no regrets about buying the car. She liked having a good-running vehicle on the place. She was strengthened by the sight of her name on the registration papers. Lately, she'd had the strange sensation she was disappearing, fading quietly, like an old bruise. Seeing her name on anything, she thought, might slow down the process.

By the time Eva got her sweater on and started down the walk, Margaret had already hauled a bag of groceries from the back seat and was lugging it and a family-size jug of Clorox toward the house. Margaret was a big, sad-faced girl, with sallow skin. Unlike Eva, who was petite and had always considered herself quite feminine, Margaret looked like the type of woman who would be good at building fence. It was this largeness of person, Eva had long suspected, that hurt Margaret's chances for remarriage.

Eva had given birth to her daughter late in life. She would have had children earlier if she'd been able and more after Margaret if she could have, but her doctor told her shortly after Margaret was born that more babies at her age could kill her, to which Lloyd replied he thought it was worth the risk. He wanted a son.

"I'll cook for you. I'll wash for you. I'll even share my

great-granddaddy's farm with you. But I'm not about to die for you, Lloyd Duncan," Eva told him. "Who'd look after Margaret?"

So Eva fixed a bed upstairs and left Lloyd downstairs by himself. She let him visit her one night a month when she was sure it was safe, but after six months Lloyd lost interest. "It's hard to get enthused," he said, sadly, "when you know it's all going to come to naught."

Despite Margaret's size, Eva was proud of her daughter. She was especially proud that Margaret had enrolled in college. Eva came from an educated family herself—all her people had finished high school, and they were all great readers. Here she was with a daughter who had gone beyond. It was a sign, she thought, of hope and possibility. There had been times in recent years when she had sat in her rocking chair on the back porch in the evening, gazed at her sagging gray barn and thought: Eva Duncan, you are witnessing the end of something. You are a caboose at the end of a runaway train. Having a daughter in college clearly proved to her this was not the case.

And it was nice, Eva had to admit, to be able to send Christmas cards that said, "Margaret is going to college now. She is just taking a few classes, but she is gearing up for a full load and a degree. I think she has it in her to make a artist."

Even if Margaret never learned enough to paint a picture good enough to give to relatives or to hang in the living room, Eva hoped college would result in remarriage for her daughter and grandbabies galore for herself. She craved the chatter of children on her place. She could die a happy woman, she often thought, if only she could hold the sixth generation in her arms.

It was Eva's impression that college men paid less attention to a woman's looks and focused more on the quality of her mind. The few college men Eva had known all had ugly wives. "Please let her meet some nice fella who ain't afraid of hard work and who doesn't have a temper," Eva prayed. "And it would be nice," she said, "if he had a truck with racks so we could go to the stock sale once in a while and pick us up some calves."

"I'll settle for a aggerculture major or a forster," Eva had told Margaret during preregistration.

"They don't have those majors at this college, Mama," Margaret had replied. "You want something like that, you got to send me up to the university."

They'd laughed afterwards, each leaving room for the possibility she might be kidding. Eva was not.

Standing midway between the house and car, Eva watched her daughter carry groceries up the walk. "Here, hon," she said, pulling on the Clorox, reaching for the grocery sack. "That's way too heavy for one person to carry."

"I got it, Mama," said Margaret.

"Give it here," said Eva, tugging. "Let me help."

"I said I got it."

"You'll strain your back. Tip your uterus. You'll end up like that Kemper woman and never be able to have any kids."

Without a word, Margaret let go of the jug of Clorox, and it hit the ground and sat like an innovative lawn decoration in the yard.

Eva opened her mouth and started to say something, but the distance between her mouth and brain had suddenly grown quite large. She was annoyed with herself for spoiling a perfectly good evening, but lately, she couldn't seem to help it. She stepped off the walk and stood ankle-deep in a patch of henbit as she watched her daughter pass. She lifted her hands in a helping gesture as if she were the one carrying the load, but the gesture, even to her, seemed feeble and useless. She tried to remember why she had come out the walk in the first place. There was something she wanted to say, something she had been angry or upset about, but as usual, whatever it was had escaped her—seeped out of her skull, floated upward and disappeared like wisps of wood smoke in the clear spring air.

Eva and her daughter sat down to supper in silence, which was no different from the way they usually went about it. They weren't mad at each other about anything Eva knew of; they'd just lived together long enough to know everything the other thought. Still, Eva preferred conversation to a lack of it. And she did think her daughter seemed unusually quiet about something this evening.

"Are we mad at each other?" she said.

Margaret crumbled crackers in her bowl and stirred her soup. "Not that I know of, Mama." She sighed.

After a while, Margaret looked at her mother and frowned. "What is this?" she said, tapping her bowl with her spoon.

"Soup," said Eva, smiling.

"Hmmm. What's in it?"

"Lots of things," said Eva, still smiling. She was hoping her persistent cheerfulness would draw attention away from the embarrassing fact that she truly could not remember. She could remember where she was and what she was doing when the Japanese attacked Pearl Harbor and what she was wearing July 13, 1945, the first time Lloyd came to court her, but she hadn't found anyone lately who wanted to hear about that. From all indications, stories about the past were as tiresome to Margaret as having to put up with the drunks who waved to her every morning at the back entrance to the court-house from their windows in the county jail.

Margaret scooted her chair back from the table, went to the cupboard where she found a jar of peanut butter, and fixed herself a sandwich.

"Your Daddy used to have little down spells," said Eva.

"Is that what I'm having, Mama? A little down spell?"

"He had 'em every few days. He'd be going along fine and—boom!—one'd hit him. Going along fine, everything under control and—boom!—there'd come another one." Eva stared out the window. "He was a hard man to figure out."

"Not really," said Margaret, "if you think about it."

Eva regarded her daughter. "I don't want to think about it," she said. "It's spring, and I want to think happy thoughts. I want to think about having my roof fixed, getting my yard in shape, and planting my garden. But I can't think about any of that until you tell me what's the matter. I still say you're mad at me about something. I'm your mama. I can tell."

"I'm not mad," said Margaret. "I'm just having myself a little down spell. I was going along fine, everything under control, then I came home and—boom!—something hit me."

Eva shook her head. "You're just depressed. You're feeling sorry for yourself. What have you got to be sorry about, a big, healthy girl like you? Just look at all you've been given: a home, a job, a mother who loves you."

"I'm thirty-eight," said Margaret.

"Yes, said Eva, proudly, "and I remember the night you were born."

"Sometimes I wish you'd forget."

Eva stared at her daughter as if she'd just come home. "You *are* depressed," she said, and the realization rose light as an arrow inside her and settled in her heart like a stone.

She pursed her lips and looked at her reflection in the china cabinet. She tried to think of an interesting or amusing bit of news to tell. Every evening, she made an effort to have at least one tidbit to share with her daughter, one morsel she had gleaned from the day's events that would make her daughter laugh again, make her marvel at the world the way she had when she was a child. But lately, Margaret had lost her marveling knack. She didn't seem to care that six deer had wandered off the hill behind the garden and had stood at least ten minutes in plain view of the house or that the Equitable Natural Gas truck had passed by around noon with somebody new inside it. Just yesterday, Eva had toyed with the idea of making up a spectacular tale and pretending it had really happened, but she was afraid of the spiritual consequences of lying at her age, with such a short amount of time left on earth to make amends. Lying had never come naturally to her. Tonight, it suddenly occurred to her, she wouldn't have to.

Eva put her spoon down, folded her hands in her lap, and cleared her throat.

Margaret chewed her sandwich and stared at the floor.

"Your mother has been in an earthquake," Eva confided. Earlier, she'd planned to withhold the information and serve it like pudding at the end of the meal, but, like pudding, the news was best served hot, she supposed, before it cooled and got a skin on it. She waited for a reaction. "Well? Aren't you even going to ask where?"

"Where?" said Margaret. She flattened her sandwich, took another bite, and listened with the enthusiasm of one who has heard bigger tales at the courthouse.

"Here, for Heaven's sake!" said Eva, rapping her knuckles on the table. "Right here on my own land." She was surprised to find that in the few hours that had elapsed, her fear of the event had been replaced by a sense of pride in having sur-

vived it. And though she was sure she wanted no more earthquakes on her farm, the one she'd experienced had somehow
made her feel a part of the world again, and the feeling was
both exhilarating and frightening and a little like riding in the
car with Margaret into town.

"How come I didn't hear anything about it?" said Margaret.

"Why, it was all over the radio. If you'd been close to a
radio, you would have."

Margaret shrugged. "I listened to the radio all the way
home, Mama. If there'd been an earthquake, I think I would
have heard."

Eva frowned and looked at her daughter. "Maybe not," she
said. "You might have missed it when you stopped at the
store or something."

"Maybe," said Margaret. "But I don't think so."

Eva began to feel a tightening in her chest as though her
ribs were being crowded. "I'm not saying you *did*. I'm just
saying you *could* have. OK? What other explanation could
there be?"

"Beats me," said Margaret. "All I know is I come home
after a long day, my mother meets me on the walk and jerks
the groceries out of my hand, fixes soup and doesn't remember what's in it, then swears she's been in an earthquake.
Honestly, Mama." Shaking her head, Margaret picked up her
bowl and headed into the kitchen.

Eva sat there a moment and stared at her soup as though
she were looking into a well. She backtracked and tried to
figure out where the conversation had gone wrong. "I would
never have talked to my mother that way," she said to herself.

"No, because I wouldn't have allowed it," said a familiar
voice inside her head.

"Oh, Mama," Eva said, fondly. Lately, she was having trouble telling the difference between mothers and daughters. They had melded at some point when her back was turned, lost their distinction, run together.

Later that evening, Eva sat alone in the living room eating a bowl of Grape-Nuts and watching "Gunsmoke" while Margaret got ready to go back into town. Since Margaret had talked her into buying a satellite dish, Eva could see old episodes of some of her favorite programs, and she was always as surprised to see Matt Dillon's face on the screen after so many years as she would've been to see Lloyd return from the grave.

This evening, Festus was in the Long Branch talking to Miss Kitty. Eva pointed her finger at Miss Kitty as though she were going to shoot her. "You," she said, "wear way too much makeup."

Dressed in jeans and a black sweater, Margaret passed back and forth through the living room getting ready. Her boot heels left little holes like chicken pox scars in the pile of the carpet. Eva didn't approve of her daughter going out at night, a woman out alone at night didn't look right, she thought, but Margaret already knew what she thought, so there was no point in saying it. "Black ain't your color, either. Black is for widows and harlots," she wanted to say, but she'd already said that a time or two, as well, so she filled her mouth with cereal to avoid temptation.

She was sitting there munching and minding her own business when an important thought occurred to her. "Ummmm," she said. She put her hand on her chest as though something pained her. She was afraid her important thought would be gone before she was ready to release it. She could see it disappearing down some dark hole like a piece of unchewed food. "Ummmm," she said again, chewing, and she was worn out by the time she was able to speak. "When's that boy from Disneyland coming to fix my house? We wait too much longer, the ceilings'll start to rot."

Margaret bent at the waist, flipped her head forward until the top half of her was upside down, then began to brush her thin, shoulder-length hair. Already, she had a significant amount of gray and looking at it filled Eva with a perplexing sense of guilt. "He's not from Disneyland, Mama. He used to live in California, that's all. I talked to him yesterday, and he said he was going to come by any day now and take a look at the roof."

"I'm not paying him to *look* at it," said Eva. "I want him to *fix* it." She stared at her daughter's mouth, surprised at how unfamiliar her own child could look upside down. She remembered a game she used to play with her sister, Marie. One of them would hang upside down from the bottom limb of the maple tree in the front yard, and they would giggle and laugh trying to imagine the upper lip as the lower. Lately, the world seemed upside down. Upside down and splitting open at the seams. Thinking about it only gave Eva a headache and made her lose track of what she was thinking. What was she thinking? Marie. Whatever happened to Marie?

"Dead," said Marie.

"What's that?" said Margaret.

Eva looked at her daughter.

"You were saying something about Aunt Marie."

"Not me," said Eva. "I deny it."

Margaret straightened slowly and stared at her mother. Her hair stood out from her head like two starched wings. "Oh, Mama," she said, shaking her head sadly. "What's happening to you?"

Eva blinked. "Oh, Margaret," she said. "What's happening to you?"

Margaret sighed. She put on her sweater and dug in her purse for her keys.

"You interested in him?" said Eva.

"Who?"

"Walt's boy," said Eva. "Who else."

"I'm not gonna tell you that, Mama. I tell you that, it'll be just like last time. You'll find something the matter with him. Ears too big. Wrong last name. Something. You'll worry yourself sick and threaten to have a heart attack."

"I never did that," said Eva. She thought a moment. "Did I do that?"

"You certainly did." Margaret picked up her purse and sweater and started toward the door.

"Don't I get a kiss? What if I was to die before you get back?"

Margaret stopped in the doorway with her back to her mother. One hand rested on the door facing in what could have been the gesture of a woman trying to prevent a wall from caving in. Slowly, she turned around, came back, and gave her a kiss. "Don't wait up for me, Mama."

Eva shut her eyes and clung to her daughter's neck. The next thing she knew, Margaret was taillights disappearing around a bend.

Eva sat in her chair and stared at the TV. She tried to think of some work to do: clothes that needed mending, laundry to fold or iron. All work and no play had kept her a young woman. No work and all play only made her sleepy. In less than five minutes, she was dreaming.

She dreamed she was a child again, and the farm was one of the biggest, most productive in the county. Dreams had a way of doing that lately: turning time back, washing the house and yard in a rich, butter-colored light, flattering the people who lived there. The farm hands went about their work, sunburnt, bib-overalled, whistling in the barnlot. "Why, I know you!" Eva called to them, and they smiled and waved to her.

Trees moved back over the hills like receding hairlines; fences rose from rotting heaps, their chestnut rails zig-zagging across the pasture like old bones. Creeks began to run in the hollows again—trickles at first, then louder, carving holes deep enough for Eva to swim in, clear enough for her to see crawcrabs waving their pincers as they scooted over the rocks on the bottom. She had just sat down in a sunny patch of squaw weed along the creek bank and was about to take off her shoes and swish her feet in the water, when she noticed a herd of sleek, rust-colored cattle running through a field. Suddenly, as though guided by a shift in the wind, they changed direction and came thundering straight at her. She tried to run, but to her surprise, her feet were stuck in mud. She covered her head with her arms to protect herself from hundreds of stamping hooves, and it was while she was waiting to be trampled that she knew what she needed to say to save herself. The words had been there, on the tip of her tongue, all along. Strangely enough, they were the same words she'd wanted to say to Margaret earlier that evening out on the walk, and she remembered them just as the cattle were upon her. "Slow down!" she yelled until her lungs ached. "Slow down, slow down, slow down!" she cried until her chest felt hollow. She was amazed that the cow that skidded to a stop in front of her ran on wheels and smelled of burning rubber.

        His name was Al, and he was an artist. "He's just working on houses till he can get through college," said Margaret.

Eva had never met a real artist, unless she counted Margaret—which she did not—but she didn't anticipate being impressed. "What kind of man goes around daddy-dabbing with a little brush?" she wanted to ask. Instead, she kept quiet. She'd had a relatively pleasant week, and if it turned otherwise, she didn't want anyone to say she was to blame. Common sense told her she ought to take charge and call Claude. Her fingers twitched every time she looked at the phone. "Are you the woman of the house or aren't you?" she asked herself each morning as she stood in front of her dresser mirror.

Margaret's friend had told her he'd be by to take a look at the roof on Saturday. It was Saturday, and Margaret was supposed to pick him up at Meacham's Restaurant in town at nine o'clock. Eva stood in the kitchen leaning against the sink and warming her bones in the sunlight that streamed through the window. A fine day for roof patching, she would've said, but she had awakened with a strange ringing noise like an alarm going off inside her head. It clanged so loudly she put her hands to her temples. "I think I'm coming down with something," she said. She waited for some expression of sympathy from her daughter, some sign that her physical discomfort was important enough to merit a change of plans, but Margaret, who was putting on lipstick in front of the bathroom mirror, put a piece of toilet paper between her lips to remove the excess, and pretended not to have heard a word her mother had said.

Outside, the sunlight cut into the fog, routed it out of the hollows, and warmed the earth until it steamed. It was hot enough to have the kitchen door open.

"How come he doesn't have a car?" said Eva, massaging her temples. "If he's so good at what he does, how come he goes around on foot? You'd think Walt Disney, with all his money, would see to it his boy had a car. The old skinflint."

Margaret filled both cheeks with air, then let it out until her breath fogged the glass. "In the first place, Mama, Walt Disney is dead, so he can't see to anything. In the second place, this guy never has been, isn't, and never will be Walt Disney's son. And thirdly, if I'd known you were going to work yourself into a tizzy over nothing, I would've let the roof cave in on both our heads before I lifted a finger."

"OK," said Eva, holding her hands up. "I'm not gonna argue with you. I just think you should've told me, that's all. There are things I like to know about a person before I hire him." One of Eva's cats meowed and clawed its way up the screen. Eva folded her arms and leaned toward the cat. "I didn't know he didn't have a car," she said to it, as though explaining her choice of hired help to a jury. "Claude Ferguson has a car. A car and one of those work trucks with big, wooden boxes on the back so he can carry his gadgets and tools right with him." Until now, Eva had not been aware of the respect she had for Claude. She was overcome by a feeling of affection for him, which feeling she ordinarily would have kept in cold-storage until his death. If Claude Ferguson ever wrecked his work truck, and she was the first person to happen along, she knew exactly what the inside of him would look like if those insides were spilled all over the highway. There were no surprises with a man like Claude.

While Margaret went to town, Eva cleaned the burners on the stove, swept the kitchen, and pulled hair clogs from the bathroom sink. She began to worry what people in town might think if they saw her daughter in Meacham's Restaurant so early in the morning with this Al. It looked intimate, no doubt about it, and Eva was afraid the story would be all over town. She'd seen reputations ruined by less.

She was debating whether or not to call the restaurant and explain to Katy Meacham that the man with Margaret was only going to spread tar and hammer nails, nothing more, when she heard the dogs growl, looked out the window, and saw her K-Car approaching the house at a rapid rate of speed—this time with two people inside it.

Eva hurried into the kitchen and watched through the screen door as the car pulled into the barnlot. The man who got out on the passenger side was tall, more than six feet, dressed in a T-shirt and jeans. Though he towered over Margaret, he was no wider than the post that held Eva's dinner bell. The widest thing about him was his hair, which was blond and curly, and if he hadn't moved, Eva, at that distance, might easily have mistaken him for an early-bloom variety of sunflower.

A hippie, Eva said to herself, and the thought gave her a sharp pain in her head. The hippies had infiltrated the county in recent years. They had drifted in, a few at a time, in beat-up vans with license plates that said "New York," "Michigan," and "California." They bought land up hollows and had babies out of wedlock, then saddled those babies with names like "Moonbeam," "Snowflake," and "Mulberry." Eva knew all about the hippies. She'd heard everything she needed to know at church. Now she'd gone and hired one, and before she knew what was happening, she had him on her porch.

"Mama, this is Al," said Margaret. The expression on Margaret's face reminded Eva of the way people look when they have their picture put in the county paper alongside big fish they've caught or ten-point bucks.

Eva stared at the man through the screen door. "Al what?" she said.

He looked at Margaret.

"Al-an, Al-bert, Al-what?" said Eva.

He smiled. "Just Al."

"What's your family name?"

"Mama!" said Margaret.

"Nice to meet you," said Eva.

"Hey," the man said. He opened the screen door, and whether it was intentional or not—Eva couldn't tell—he greeted her by shaking her thumb.

"I'm going to fix Al some tea, Mama," said Margaret, and as she eased through the door past her mother, she shot her a warning glance. "Would you like some tea, Mama?"

"I don't like tea," said Eva. "You know that." She continued to stare at the man. He was younger than Margaret, she guessed, and had skin as pale as a cave cricket, a characteristic she deemed worth pointing out later to her daughter. His arms were covered with soft-looking white down, and even that looked unearned. "I have more hair on my upper lip than you have on your entire body," Eva said to herself. Lloyd had been quite hairy. He'd had thick chest hair that didn't run out of steam when it crossed his shoulders, but extended down his back like a vest. This man in her yard could easily have passed for some new species. The earth splits open, thought Eva, and you are what crawls out.

"So," said Al, hands on his skinny hips, looking around. "This is some place you've got here." There was an easy, slow-motion quality about his voice that hit Eva's ears and was instantly decoded to mean: All my life I've been wandering, now I'm tired and looking for a place to lie down. "You have any idea how old this house is?" he said.

Eva squinted at him. She spied a gold ring in his ear. "Older'n you," she said.

"Ha!" said Al. "That's a good one! I'll have to remember

that. Older than me. I like that." Nodding, he sat down in Eva's willow rocker and ran his hands slowly up and down the arms of the chair. "I have a thing for old houses," he said.

Eva raised an eyebrow.

"Really," he said, holding his hands up in protest. "I have a lot of respect for old houses. When I get enough money saved, I plan to buy a spread like this, off by myself."

Eva folded her arms in front of her chest. "Save hard. Land ain't cheap."

Al smiled. He closed his eyes and leaned his head against the rocker. "Just me and the crows. No one but me and the crows for miles."

Eva's heartbeat quickened, and she felt as though a hummingbird were trapped inside her chest. She recalled stories she'd read, newscasts she'd seen about entire families slaughtered. "We ain't as alone as we look," she informed him. "You might not know this, but the woods are full of people: hunters, neighbors out for a stroll. One good thing about having neighbors is that there's always one within shouting range."

Al opened his gray eyes and looked at her. "Is that a fact? Goes to show you what you don't see when you aren't looking for it. I just remarked to Margie on the way up the road how long it's been since I was truly alone in nature."

"You're never alone in nature," said Margaret, returning with a glass of iced tea. She set the tea on a flower stand beside the rocker.

Eva looked at the two of them and frowned as though she'd missed something. "What in thunder are you talking about?"

"Oh, Mama," said Margaret. She laughed.

"What are you laughing at?" said Al. "Is that any way to show respect for your mother?"

"See here," said Eva. She was about to tell him she'd decide when to chastise her own daughter, but before she had a chance, he grabbed Margaret, hooked her head under his arm, and, briskly, began to rub her scalp with his knuckles.

Margaret struggled, her laughter easy and free. Eva watched them stagger off the porch and into the yard, and she could not rid herself of the notion she'd missed something. She felt as if an important decision had been made, and she had not been consulted. "Here!" she said. She opened the screen door and followed them as they wrestled around the yard. "That's enough now. Someone's gonna get hurt!" She tried to grab the man's arms, and when she couldn't, she looked around for a broom or stick to separate them. Finding neither, she began to pound her fists on the man's back. "Stop that!" she shouted.

"Whoooaaa!" he said, turning Margaret loose. "Look out!" He jumped back and waved both hands in the air in an exaggerated gesture of surrender. Eyes closed tightly, Eva continued to pummel him. She stood, in the shadow of her father's house, and fought bravely to defend what belonged to her. She hit him once on the side of his head, and instantly, her eyes flew open. She stared at her throbbing hand, then at Al and Margaret, then at her hand again as if she couldn't believe what it had done. There was a moment of awkward silence.

Looking surprised and more than a little perplexed, Al rubbed his head and sat down on the ground.

"What on earth!" said Margaret. She bent over Al and checked his head as if she expected to see blood.

"I didn't mean—," said Eva. She looked about her, defensively, like the mother of an ornery child who has just committed a particularly heinous act. "For Heaven's sake," she said. "I barely hit him."

"That's not the point!" shouted Margaret.

"What did you expect me to do? Stand here and let him hurt you?"

"He wasn't hurting me, Mama."

"How was I to know that?" Eva snapped. She looked at her daughter. Margaret's cheeks were flushed. Her skin had temporarily lost its sallowness, and she looked more alive than Eva had seen her in years.

Eva headed up the walk. She stopped on the porch steps, turned around and glared at Al. "See what you've done!"

"He hasn't done a thing!" said Margaret.

Eva folded her arms. "That's right! He's been here half an hour, and he hasn't done a thing!" Eva came back out the walk and stopped in front of Al. "Are you here to fix my roof or not?"

Al shrugged.

"Of course he is," said Margaret.

"Fine!" Eva said. "Then fix it! There's a ladder in the barn and a bucket of sealant in the cellar. Take that sealant and daub it over the holes in the roof. When you're finished, holler, and I'll pay you. Then I want you off my place. Understand?"

"Sure," said Al, smiling at Margaret. "I understand."

Eva plodded up the walk. On the porch, she stopped and said to her daughter without turning around: "Come inside and eat your breakfast."

"I've already eaten, Mama. Remember?"

Eva opened the screen door. "Good," she said. "Come on inside and eat again."

Eva stood by the mantel in the living room and waited for Margaret to come into the house. She leaned her back against the wall for support and tried to ignore the pain in her heart. When Margaret appeared in the doorway from the dining room, Eva grabbed her daughter and put her hand over her mouth. They struggled briefly, and in the process, Eva almost fell.

"Stop this!" said Margaret, prying her mother off her. "What's the matter with you?"

"I don't know what you think you're doing," said Eva, her breath coming in short, hard gasps, "but you'd better come to your senses!"

Margaret jerked her arm away. "I'm not the one who seems to have turned loose of my senses!" she shouted. She stared at her mother, then shook her head and went out into the hall.

"Listen to me!" said Eva, following her. "You have no idea what we're dealing with. That man is dangerous."

Margaret put her face so close to Eva's it was impossible to tell whether she intended to kiss or bite her. "Dangerous for who, Mama? Me or *you?*"

Outside, the ladder thumped against the side of the house. It squeaked rhythmically as Al began to climb the rungs, and in the squeaking, Eva heard the unmistakable sounds of desecration. "Listen," she said. "You've got to listen. You remember that earthquake I told you about?"

"Oh, Mama," said Margaret. She looked out the window and laughed bitterly.

"Laugh if you want to," said Eva, "but there's a connection. I just haven't had time to figure it out. We never had an earthquake around here before. We never had people like him, either. It's a sign of something. You're a smart girl. You've had math. You figure it out."

Margaret stared out the hall window as if she were seeing

something besides the ruins of the calf lot across the creek. Slowly, her eyes filled with tears. "Not smart enough, Mama, or it wouldn't have taken me this long to figure certain things out."

"What things? What are you talking about?"

Margaret lifted the bottom of her shirt and used it to wipe her eyes. Without another word, she turned and went outside.

"What things?" shouted Eva. She stood for a few seconds with her hand on the banister, then looked at the pictures of her ancestors on the walls. "What things?" she asked them.

When Al came off the roof at eleven, Eva quietly got her purse and started out onto the back porch to pay him. "He's not finished, Mama," said Margaret from the kitchen.

"Yes, he is," said Eva.

"Put your purse away, Mama. He doesn't want your money."

Eva went into the kitchen. "What does he want then?"

Margaret stood in front of the sink mixing hamburger, oats, and ketchup in a bowl. "At the moment, he wants his dinner, Mama. A working man's got to eat."

Eva refused to join them. During dinner, she sat on the porch in her rocker and listened to the dogs under the house scratch their fleas. From where she sat, she could look through the screen door into the dining room. It was strange to see a man at her table after so many years. She was surprised to discover how little she had missed the sight.

An early afternoon wind, as gentle and sweet as a mother's breath, fanned her face and neck. Eva closed her eyes. She was in the habit of taking a short nap this time of day and despite her unhappiness, she found herself drifting. In the darkness behind her lids, she saw a baby. It crawled around for awhile, then stopped and reached for her, drooling. She was about to pick it up when she noticed more babies crawling from under her house. Instead of being fat and pink, they were as pale and hairless as new pigs, and each one had a gold ring in its ear.

Eva got out of her chair and stood on the steps. Waving her hands, she tried to drive the babies back under the house. She'd just get one to go under, and a dozen more would crawl out. They rooted in the cool dirt, wallowed at her feet, and made little grunting noises as they tried to climb her legs. "Get back!" Eva said, kicking. One climbed all the way to her waist, and, in horror, she flung it from her. She was about to call for help when she noticed the ladder leaning against the house. Eva made a dash for it. The next thing she knew, her foot was on the bottom rung.

Though she'd done a lot of walking in her day, she'd never had much strength in her legs. By the time she passed the first-story windows, her legs were trembling. She kept her eyes on the point far above where roof and ladder met sky, and she stopped only once and looked down to make sure she wasn't being followed. She had no idea what she planned to do when she got to the top, but it gave her strength knowing she'd be doing the deciding.

When she reached the roof, she climbed over the last rung, and with all her might, kicked the ladder sideways. She heard a scraping sound as it slid along the tin, then a loud bang. The ladder crashed into the lawn chairs, bounced once, and lay like a silver bridge across the walk. Immediately, a door slammed, and Eva heard voices on the porch. If they tried to come after her, she'd kick the ladder down again, she told herself. She'd stay up here all night, for the rest of her life if she had to.

She scooted away from the edge, sat back and gave herself a chance to catch her breath. Shading her eyes from the sun, she gazed east to what used to be the apple orchard hill. She could see where the cleared land used to be. There was a definite line where the big oaks she had played under as a child stopped and the small trees and brush began. From this height, it was easy to tell the difference between now and then.

Below her, she could hear her daughter calling. Though the sun beat down upon Eva's head, her face was cooled by a rising wind. She folded the skirt of her dress under her to keep the tin from burning her skin, then crossed her bony legs and treated herself to the view. Here was a world she recognized, and she was impressed by the orderliness of it. Yard running into pasture, pasture leading into hills, hills fading into distant mountains. Clearly, it was a world without end.

PS
3561
.O354
F37
1990

91-249

Gramley Library
Salem Academy and College
Winston-Salem, N.C. 27108

Gramley Library
Salem Academy and College
Winston-Salem, N.C. 27108